time to cook

great
meals

in 10, 20 & 30 minutes

p

This is a Parragon Book
This edition published in 2005

Parragon
Queen Street House
4 Queen Street
Bath BA1 1HE, UK

ISBN: 1-40543-018-4

Printed in Indonesia

Produced by the Bridgewater Book Company Ltd.

Note
This book uses metric and imperial measurements. Follow the same
units of measurement throughout; do not mix metric and imperial.
All spoon measurements are level: teaspoons are assumed to be 5 ml,
and tablespoons are assumed to be 15 ml. Unless otherwise stated, milk
is assumed to be full fat, eggs and individual vegetables such as potatoes
are medium, and pepper is freshly ground black pepper.

The nutritional information provided for each recipe is per serving or per
person. Optional ingredients, variations or serving suggestions have not
been included in the calculations. The times given for each recipe are an
approximate guide only, because the preparation times may differ
according to the techniques used by different people and the cooking
times may vary as a result of the type of oven used.

Recipes using raw or very lightly cooked eggs should be avoided by
infants, the elderly, pregnant women, convalescents, and anyone
suffering from an illness. Pregnant and breastfeeding women are
advised to avoid eating peanuts and peanut products.

Key to symbols used in this book

 Preparation time

 Cooking time

 Serving number

Contents

10
20
30

Introduction

You don't have to slave over the proverbial hot stove to create fabulous food for family meals and to entertain friends – at least, not any more. This book is packed with mouthwatering recipes that can be both prepared and cooked in minutes. All the dishes in the first chapter take a maximum of 10 minutes, those in the second a maximum of 20 minutes and those in the third a maximum of 30 minutes.

Many of the dishes can be ready and on the table in the time it takes to prepare a supermarket ready meal. The difference is that what you see before you on the plate will match the photograph on the page, the meal will have the irresistible flavour of fresh cooking, and you will be able to take pleasure in your cooking skills.

The secret of successful fast food is being well organized and thinking ahead. If you need the oven or grill for a recipe, switch it on to preheat before you even start collecting your ingredients together – and do gather up everything you need before you begin to cook. Once you're whizzing through a recipe, there won't be time to rummage around in the back of a cupboard for a can of tomatoes or in a drawer for a roll of foil. Keep knives sharp so that you can chop or slice ingredients into even-sized pieces quickly. This also makes it easier to slice thinly or chop finely, both of which will speed up the cooking process. A set of different-sized pans is essential and if they are heavy-based, food is far less likely to scorch, freeing you to get on with some other part of the recipe while the first ingredients are cooking. When it comes to useful kitchen tools, a hand-held blender is invaluable as you can purée soups and sauces while they're still in the saucepan.

All three chapters of this book include dishes for all courses and occasions and every season of the year, from soups and appetizers to desserts and from exquisite salads to satisfying pasta. As well as not having to invest huge amounts of your time in preparing great dishes, you don't have to invest huge amounts of money either. Elegant simplicity is the keynote of many of these recipes, although there are some luxurious ingredients for those times you really want to push the boat out.

The following pages will take you around the world in no more than 30 minutes as they feature great dishes from countries as diverse as China and Italy, India and Greece. All are stylish enough for easy entertaining and cater for all tastes, from creamy pâté to rich soup, spicy curry to sophisticated steak, sizzling seafood to vegetarian parcels, and refreshing fruit desserts to the most indulgent chocolate confections.

You don't have to be a celebrity chef to prepare delicious food in the wink of an eye and nor do you have to master 'plating' techniques to serve it. However, it takes very little time to present food in an appetizing way, arranging it attractively on the plates so that it looks as good as it tastes. Fresh herbs, either chopped or in sprigs, always make pretty garnishes and wedges of lemon or lime go well

with many fish and seafood dishes. Colourful salad leaves, such as radicchio and oak leaf lettuce, make a quick and pleasing accompaniment or a simple garnish. Croûtons and lardons, available from supermarkets, give that extra touch to soups, as does a simple swirl of cream.

Whether you are planning an alfresco lunch with friends, a celebratory dinner party or just a delicious family supper, it's easy to be a great cook – with great dishes and great timing.

5

10 minutes to cook

One of the secrets to cooking in 10 minutes is to be organized. Make sure you have all of your ingredients and equipment ready before you begin cooking, then it will be very easy to create a delicious and healthy dish in a matter of minutes.

10

10 MINUTES TO COOK   Hummus

This mildly spicy Middle Eastern dip is easy to make and tastes much better than shop-bought brands. Serve with crudités such as carrot, celery, red pepper batons, and breadsticks.

Nutritional Information
Calories 340
Protein 13g
Carbohydrate 17g
Sugars 1g
Fat 25g
Saturates 3g

INGREDIENTS

425 g/15 oz canned chickpeas, drained and rinsed

125 ml/4 fl oz tahini

3 garlic cloves, crushed

125 ml/4 fl oz lemon juice

3–4 tbsp water

salt and pepper

TO GARNISH

1 tbsp olive oil

pinch of cayenne pepper

1 tbsp chopped fresh parsley

6 whole black olives

1 Mix the chickpeas, tahini, garlic and lemon juice together in a bowl and beat in enough water to make a smooth paste. Season to taste with salt and pepper. Alternatively, place the chickpeas, tahini, garlic, lemon juice and 3 tablespoons of the water in a food processor, season to taste with salt and pepper and process until a smooth paste forms. If the mixture is too thick, add a little more water.

2 Transfer the hummus to a serving dish and make a shallow dip in the centre with the back of a spoon. Pour the oil into the dip and sprinkle with cayenne pepper. Garnish with the chopped parsley and olives. Serve immediately or cover with clingfilm and store in the refrigerator until required.

COOK'S TIP
Tahini is a thick, oily paste made from crushed toasted sesame seeds. It is available from most large supermarkets and health food shops.

10 mins

0 mins

serves 4

Celeriac Rémoulade

Celeriac served with a rémoulade sauce – a mustard-flavoured mayonnaise – is a classically simple French dish, ideal served as a starter.

Nutritional Information
Calories 236
Protein 3g
Carbohydrate 4g
Sugars 3g
Fat 24g
Saturates 3g

INGREDIENTS

225 ml/8 fl oz mayonnaise

2 tsp lemon juice

1 tbsp Dijon mustard

salt and pepper

225 g/8 oz celeriac

1 shallot

6 lettuce leaves

snipped fresh chives, to garnish

1 Mix the mayonnaise, lemon juice and mustard together in a large bowl, then season to taste with salt and pepper. Peel and grate the celeriac into the mixture.

2 Grate the shallot and stir it in thoroughly, making sure the celeriac is well coated in the dressing.

3 Line a salad bowl with the lettuce leaves and spoon the celeriac mixture into the centre. Sprinkle with snipped chives and serve.

10 MINUTES TO COOK   Mexican Tomato Salad

This easy and economical salad makes an ideal light vegetarian lunch, served with some crusty bread, or it would be a good accompaniment to a barbecue.

Nutritional Information
Calories 210
Protein 8g
Carbohydrate 25g
Sugars 10g
Fat 9g
Saturates 1g

INGREDIENTS

**600 g/1 lb 5 oz tomatoes, peeled, deseeded
and roughly chopped**

1 onion, thinly sliced and pushed out into rings

**400 g/14 oz canned kidney beans, drained
and rinsed**

1 fresh green chilli, deseeded and thinly sliced

3 tbsp chopped fresh coriander

3 tbsp olive oil

1 garlic clove, finely chopped

4 tbsp lime juice

salt and pepper

1 Place the chopped tomatoes and onion slices into a large serving bowl and mix well. Stir in the kidney beans.

2 Mix the chilli, coriander, oil, garlic and lime juice together in a large jug and season to taste with salt and pepper.

3 Pour the dressing over the salad and toss thoroughly. Serve immediately or cover with clingfilm and leave to chill in the refrigerator until required.

VARIATION
You could substitute two canned chipotle chillies, drained and rinsed, for the fresh chilli, and broad beans for the kidney beans, if you prefer.

10 MINUTES TO COOK Warm Goat's Cheese Salad

This delicious salad combines soft goat's cheese with walnut halves, served on a bed of mixed salad leaves.

Nutritional Information
Calories 408
Protein 9g
Carbohydrate 8g
Sugars 8g
Fat 38g
Saturates 8g

INGREDIENTS

85 g/3 oz walnut halves
mixed salad leaves
125 g/4½ oz soft goat's cheese
snipped fresh chives, to garnish
DRESSING
6 tbsp walnut oil
3 tbsp white wine vinegar
1 tbsp clear honey
1 tsp Dijon mustard
pinch of ground ginger
salt and pepper

1 To make the dressing, whisk the oil, vinegar, honey, mustard and ginger together in a small saucepan. Season to taste with salt and pepper.

2 Heat the dressing gently, stirring occasionally, until warm. Add the walnut halves and continue to heat for 3–4 minutes.

3 Arrange the salad leaves on 4 serving plates and place spoonfuls of goat's cheese on top. Lift the walnut halves from the dressing with a slotted spoon and sprinkle them over the salad leaves.

4 Transfer the warm dressing to a small jug. Sprinkle chives over the salads and serve with the dressing.

COOK'S TIP
You could also use a ewe's milk cheese, such as feta, in this recipe for a slightly sharper flavour.

10 MINUTES TO COOK Flambéed Peaches

This dessert is a fabulous end to a dinner party – especially if your guests are watching you cook. It makes a luxurious but, at the same time, refreshing final course.

Nutritional Information
Calories 227
Protein 3g
Carbohydrate 26g
Sugars 26g
Fat 11g
Saturates 6g

INGREDIENTS

3 tbsp unsalted butter

3 tbsp muscovado sugar

4 tbsp orange juice

4–6 ripe peaches, peeled, halved and stoned

2 tbsp almond liqueur or peach brandy

4 tbsp toasted flaked almonds

1 Heat the butter, muscovado sugar and orange juice in a large, heavy-based frying pan over a low heat, stirring constantly, until the butter has melted and the sugar has dissolved.

2 Add the peaches and cook for 1–2 minutes on each side, until golden.

3 Add the almond liqueur and ignite with a match or taper. When the flames have died down, transfer to serving dishes, sprinkle with toasted flaked almonds and serve immediately.

COOK'S TIP
Igniting the spirit will burn off the alcohol and mellow the flavour.

10 MINUTES TO COOK

Syllabub

Wine, brandy and cream make this old-fashioned dessert wonderfully self-indulgent – and it is guaranteed to make an impression if you serve it at a dinner party.

Nutritional Information
Calories 635
Protein 3g
Carbohydrate 31g
Sugars 31g
Fat 52g
Saturates 30g

INGREDIENTS

175 ml/6 fl oz Madeira
2 tbsp brandy
grated rind of 1 lemon
125 ml/4 fl oz lemon juice
115 g/4 oz caster sugar
600 ml/1 pint double cream
10 amaretti biscuits or ratafias, crumbled
ground cinnamon, for dusting
lemon slices, to decorate

1 Whisk the Madeira, brandy, lemon rind, lemon juice and sugar in a bowl until blended.

2 Add the cream to the bowl and continue whisking until the mixture is thick in consistency.

3 Divide the biscuits between 6 long-stemmed glasses or sundae dishes. Fill each glass or dish with the syllabub mixture and leave in the refrigerator to chill until ready to serve, if desired. Dust the surface of each dessert with cinnamon and decorate with lemon slices.

COOK'S TIP
Madeira is a fortified wine from the island of the same name. It may be dry, medium or sweet. Dessert Madeira is best for this recipe – use Bual or Malmsey.

10 MINUTES TO COOK

Lemon Posset

This is a rich and self-indulgent dessert, but the sharpness of the lemon gives it a wonderfully refreshing flavour.

Nutritional Information
Calories 408
Protein 3g
Carbohydrate 17g
Sugars 17g
Fat 36g
Saturates 23g

INGREDIENTS

grated rind and juice of 1 large lemon
4 tbsp dry white wine
55 g/2 oz caster sugar
300 ml/10 fl oz double cream
2 egg whites
lemon slices, to decorate
langues de chat biscuits, to serve

1 Mix the lemon rind, lemon juice, wine and sugar together in a bowl. Stir until the sugar has dissolved. Add the cream and beat with an electric mixer until soft peaks form.

2 Whisk the egg whites in a separate, spotlessly clean, greasefree bowl until stiff, then carefully fold them into the cream mixture.

3 Spoon the mixture into tall glasses and leave to chill in the refrigerator until required. Serve decorated with lemon slices and accompanied by the langues de chat biscuits.

VARIATION

Replace the lemon with the grated rind and juice of 1 orange, decorate with orange slices and serve with amaretti biscuits, if you prefer.

50

10 MINUTES TO COOK Indian Mango Dessert

Perhaps because the main course often tends to be spicy, Indian cooks will often serve a sweet, refreshing and creamy dessert as a contrast at the end of a meal.

Nutritional Information
Calories 412
Protein 2g
Carbohydrate 15g
Sugars 15g
Fat 39g
Saturates 24g

INGREDIENTS

2 ripe mangoes

300 ml/10 fl oz double cream, plus extra to decorate

2 tsp caster sugar

1 Place a mango on a chopping board, narrow-side down, and cut a thick slice lengthways as close to the stone as possible. Turn the mango round and slice the other side as close to the stone as possible. Cut off any flesh remaining on the stone. Reserve a few unpeeled, thin mango slices for the garnish. Without cutting through the skin of the mango halves, score the flesh in the 2 thick slices in criss-cross lines about 1 cm/½ inch apart. Fold the halves inside out and slice off the cubes of flesh. Repeat with the second mango.

2 Place the mango flesh in a blender or food processor and process until a smooth purée forms.

3 Beat the cream with the sugar until stiff, then gently fold in the mango purée. Spoon into glass dishes, cover and leave to chill in the refrigerator until required. Serve decorated with extra whipped cream and the reserved mango slices.

VARIATION
Use other exotic fruits. Cut 400 g/ 14 oz guavas in half, sprinkle with lime juice and scoop out the flesh. Don't use kiwi fruit as they curdle the cream.

48

10 MINUTES TO COOK Braised Chinese Leaves

Shredded white cabbage can be used instead of Chinese leaves for this delicious braised dish.

Nutritional Information
Calories 138
Protein 6g
Carbohydrate 10g
Sugars 4g
Fat 9g
Saturates 1g

INGREDIENTS

500 g/1 lb 2 oz Chinese leaves or white cabbage

3 tbsp vegetable oil

½ tsp Szechuan peppercorns

5–6 small dried red chillies, deseeded and chopped

½ tsp salt

1 tbsp sugar

1 tbsp light soy sauce

1 tbsp rice vinegar

few drops sesame oil (optional)

1 Cut the Chinese leaves or white cabbage into thin pieces.

2 Heat the vegetable oil in a preheated wok or large frying pan. Add the Szechuan peppercorns and dried red chillies and stir for a few seconds.

3 Add the Chinese leaves to the wok and stir-fry for 1 minute.

4 Add the salt to the mixture in the wok and continue stirring for a further 1 minute.

5 Add the sugar, soy sauce and rice vinegar, blend well and cook for a further 1 minute.

6 Finally, sprinkle on the sesame oil (if using). Serve hot or cold.

10 MINUTES TO COOK

Vegetable Chop Suey

Make sure that the vegetables are all cut into pieces of a similar size in this recipe, so that they cook within the same amount of time.

Nutritional Information

Calories 155
Protein 4g
Carbohydrate 9g
Sugars 6g
Fat 12g
Saturates 2g

INGREDIENTS

1 yellow pepper, deseeded
1 red pepper, deseeded
1 carrot
1 courgette
1 fennel bulb
1 onion
55 g/2 oz mangetout
2 tbsp peanut oil
3 garlic cloves, crushed
1 tsp grated fresh root ginger
115 g/4 oz beansprouts
2 tsp light brown sugar
2 tbsp light soy sauce
125 ml/4 fl oz vegetable stock

1 Cut the peppers, carrot, courgette and fennel into thin slices. Cut the onion into quarters, then cut each quarter in half. Slice the mangetout diagonally to create the maximum surface area.

2 Heat the oil in a preheated wok. Add the garlic and ginger and stir-fry for 30 seconds. Add the onion and stir-fry for a further 30 seconds.

3 Add the peppers, carrot, courgette, fennel and mangetout to the wok and stir-fry for 2 minutes.

4 Add the beansprouts to the wok and stir in the sugar, soy sauce and stock. Reduce the heat to low and simmer for 1–2 minutes, until the vegetables are tender and coated in the sauce.

5 Transfer the vegetables and sauce to a serving dish and serve immediately.

10 MINUTES TO COOK Stir-fried Mixed Vegetables

The Chinese carefully select vegetables to achieve a harmonious balance of contrasting colours and textures.

Nutritional Information
Calories 534
Protein 14g
Carbohydrate 19g
Sugars 8g
Fat 45g
Saturates 5g

INGREDIENTS

55 g/2 oz mangetout

1 small carrot

125 g/4½ oz Chinese leaves

55 g/2 oz button mushrooms

55 g/2 oz canned bamboo shoots, drained and rinsed

3–4 tbsp vegetable oil

125 g/4½ oz beansprouts

1 tsp salt

1 tsp sugar

1 tbsp light soy sauce

few drops sesame oil (optional)

dipping sauce, to serve (optional)

1 Prepare the vegetables: top and tail the mangetout and cut the carrot, Chinese leaves, mushrooms and bamboo shoots into roughly the same shape and size as the mangetout.

2 Heat the vegetable oil in a preheated wok or large frying pan. Add the carrot and stir-fry for a few seconds.

3 Add the mangetout and Chinese leaves to the wok and stir-fry for a further 1 minute.

4 Add the beansprouts, mushrooms and bamboo shoots to the wok and continue to stir-fry for 1 minute.

5 Add the salt and sugar, continue stirring for a further 1 minute, then add the soy sauce, blending well.

6 Sprinkle the vegetables with sesame oil (if using) and serve hot or cold, with a dipping sauce, if liked, or with rice and toasted cashew nuts (see Cook's Tip).

COOK'S TIP
Put some rice on to cook while you are preparing the stir-fry. Serve the stir-fry on a bed of rice and sprinkle a few toasted cashew nuts on top for a perfectly balanced and incredibly quick meal.

10 MINUTES TO COOK

Chickpea Salad

This attractive-looking salad is ideal served as a delicious light lunch or an informal supper.

Nutritional Information
Calories 139
Protein 8g
Carbohydrate 21g
Sugars 5g
Fat 3g
Saturates 0.4g

INGREDIENTS

400 g/14 oz canned chickpeas, drained and rinsed

4 carrots

1 bunch spring onions

1 cucumber

½ tsp salt

½ tsp pepper

3 tbsp lemon juice

1 red pepper

1 Place the drained chickpeas in a large salad bowl.

2 Using a sharp knife, peel and slice the carrots. Cut the spring onions into thin strips. Cut the cucumber into quarters lengthways and slice thickly. Add the carrots, spring onions and cucumber to the chickpeas and mix well.

3 Season with the salt and pepper and sprinkle with the lemon juice.

4 Using 2 serving spoons, gently toss the salad ingredients together.

5 Deseed and slice the red pepper into thin strips.

6 Arrange the slices of red pepper on top of the salad. Serve the salad immediately or leave to chill in the refrigerator and serve when required.

10 MINUTES TO COOK

Garlic Spaghetti

This easy and satisfying Roman dish originated as a cheap meal for the impoverished, but is now a favourite in Italian restaurants and trattorias.

Nutritional Information
Calories 477
Protein 0.6g
Carbohydrate 37g
Sugars 1.8g
Fat 40g
Saturates 3g

INGREDIENTS

125 ml/4 fl oz olive oil

3 garlic cloves, crushed

salt and pepper

450 g/1 lb fresh spaghetti

3 tbsp roughly chopped fresh parsley

1 Reserve 1 teaspoon of the oil and heat the remainder in a medium-sized saucepan over a low heat. Add the garlic and a pinch of salt, stirring constantly, until golden brown, then remove the saucepan from the heat. Do not allow the garlic to burn as it will taint the flavour of the oil. (If it does burn, you will have to start all over again!)

2 Meanwhile, bring a large saucepan of lightly salted water to the boil. Add the pasta and remaining oil, return to the boil and cook for 2–3 minutes, or until tender but still firm to the bite. Drain the pasta thoroughly and return to the saucepan.

3 Add the olive oil and garlic mixture to the pasta and toss to coat thoroughly. Season with pepper to taste, add the chopped parsley and toss well to coat.

4 Transfer the pasta to 4 warmed serving dishes and serve immediately.

COOK'S TIP
It is worth buying the best-quality olive oil. Extra virgin oil is produced from the first pressing and has the lowest acidity. It is more expensive than other types of olive oil, but has the finest flavour.

10 MINUTES TO COOK

Warm Goat's Cheese Salad

This delicious salad combines soft goat's cheese with walnut halves, served on a bed of mixed salad leaves.

Nutritional Information
Calories 408
Protein 9g
Carbohydrate 8g
Sugars 8g
Fat 38g
Saturates 8g

INGREDIENTS

85 g/3 oz walnut halves
mixed salad leaves
125 g/4½ oz soft goat's cheese
snipped fresh chives, to garnish
DRESSING
6 tbsp walnut oil
3 tbsp white wine vinegar
1 tbsp clear honey
1 tsp Dijon mustard
pinch of ground ginger
salt and pepper

1 To make the dressing, whisk the oil, vinegar, honey, mustard and ginger together in a small saucepan. Season to taste with salt and pepper.

2 Heat the dressing gently, stirring occasionally, until warm. Add the walnut halves and continue to heat for 3–4 minutes.

3 Arrange the salad leaves on 4 serving plates and place spoonfuls of goat's cheese on top. Lift the walnut halves from the dressing with a slotted spoon and sprinkle them over the salad leaves.

4 Transfer the warm dressing to a small jug. Sprinkle chives over the salads and serve with the dressing.

COOK'S TIP
You could also use a ewe's milk cheese, such as feta, in this recipe for a slightly sharper flavour.

14

10 MINUTES TO COOK Prosciutto & Figs

This classic Italian starter is simplicity itself. It would be the perfect choice to begin an alfresco meal. Try to find Parma ham or San Daniele as these are the finest prosciuttos.

Nutritional Information
Calories 145
Protein 13g
Carbohydrate 10g
Sugars 10g
Fat 6g
Saturates 2g

INGREDIENTS
8 ripe fresh figs
8 thin slices of prosciutto, about 175 g/6 oz
pepper

1 Using a sharp knife, cut each fig downwards into quarters from the stalk end, but without cutting all the way through. Gently open out each fruit like a flower and place 2 on each of 4 large serving plates.

2 Arrange 2 slices of prosciutto in decorative folds beside the figs on each plate.

3 Season well with pepper and serve at room temperature, offering the pepper mill at the same time.

VARIATION
Arrange 2 slices of prosciutto on each plate and sprinkle with Parmesan cheese shavings. Add 6 olives and drizzle with vinaigrette.

10 MINUTES TO COOK Cauliflower with Greens

This is a delicious way to cook cauliflower, with a lovely texture and flavour – even without the greens.

Nutritional Information

Calories 49
Protein 2g
Carbohydrate 3g
Sugars 2g
Fat 3g
Saturates 0.5g

INGREDIENTS

175 g/6 oz cauliflower, cut into florets

1 garlic clove

½ tsp ground turmeric

1 tbsp fresh coriander root or stem

1 tbsp sunflower oil

2 spring onions, cut into 2.5-cm/1-inch pieces

125 g/4½ oz pak choi or mustard greens, tough stalks removed

1 tsp yellow mustard seeds

1 Blanch the cauliflower, then rinse under cold running water and drain. Reserve until required.

2 Grind the garlic, turmeric and coriander root together using a pestle and mortar or spice grinder.

3 Heat the oil in a preheated wok or large, heavy-based frying pan.

4 Add the spring onions to the wok and cook over a high heat for 1 minute, stirring constantly.

5 Add the pak choi and continue to stir-fry for 1 minute. Remove the mixture from the wok and keep warm until required.

6 Return the wok to the heat and add the mustard seeds. Stir until the seeds begin to pop.

7 Add the coriander mixture and the blanched cauliflower to the wok and stir until the cauliflower is thoroughly coated.

8 Transfer the cauliflower to a warmed serving plate with the reserved greens and serve immediately.

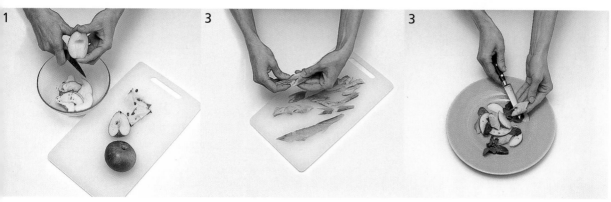

1   3   3

Smoked Trout & Apple Salad

10 MINUTES TO COOK

Smoked trout and horseradish are natural partners, but with apple and watercress this makes a wonderful first course.

Nutritional Information
Calories 133
Protein 12g
Carbohydrate 11g
Sugars 11g
Fat 5g
Saturates 1g

INGREDIENTS

2 orange-red eating apples
2 tbsp French dressing
½ bunch of watercress
1 smoked trout, about 175 g/6 oz
Melba Toast, to serve (see Cook's Tip)
HORSERADISH DRESSING
125 ml/4 fl oz low-fat natural yogurt
½–1 tsp lemon juice
1 tbsp horseradish sauce
milk (optional)
salt and pepper
TO GARNISH
1 tbsp snipped fresh chives
fresh chive flowers (optional)

1 Leaving the skin on, cut the apples into quarters and remove the cores. Slice the apples into a bowl and toss in the French dressing to prevent discoloration.

2 Break the watercress into sprigs and arrange on 4 serving plates.

3 Skin the trout and take out the bone. Carefully remove any fine bones that remain, using your fingers or tweezers. Flake the trout into fairly large pieces and arrange with the apple amongst the watercress.

4 To make the horseradish dressing, whisk all the ingredients together, adding a little milk if too thick, then drizzle over the trout. Sprinkle the snipped chives and flowers (if using) over the trout and serve with the Melba Toast (see Cook's Tip).

COOK'S TIP
To make your own Melba Toast, toast medium sliced bread, then cut off the crusts and slice in half horizontally. Cut in half diagonally and place toasted side down in a warmed oven for 15–20 minutes, until the edges curl.

Pear & Roquefort Salad

 10 mins

 0 mins

serves 4

The sweetness of the pear is a perfect partner to the peppery bite of the radicchio and the piquancy of the cheese.

Nutritional Information

Calories 94
Protein 5g
Carbohydrate 5g
Sugars 3g
Fat 4g
Saturates 3g

INGREDIENTS

55 g/2 oz Roquefort cheese
150 ml/5 fl oz low-fat natural yogurt
2 tbsp snipped fresh chives
pepper
few lollo rosso leaves
few radicchio leaves
few lamb's lettuce leaves
2 ripe pears, cored and thinly sliced
whole fresh chives, to garnish

1 Place the cheese in a bowl and mash with a fork. Gradually blend the yogurt into the cheese to make a smooth dressing. Add the chives and season with pepper to taste.

2 Arrange the salad leaves on a large serving platter or divide them between individual serving plates.

3 Arrange the pear slices over the salad leaves. Drizzle the Roquefort dressing over the pears and garnish with the whole chives.

COOK'S TIP
Look out for ready-prepared bags of mixed salad leaves as these are generally more economical than buying lots of different types separately.

30

10 MINUTES TO COOK

Chinese Omelette

This omelette contains chicken and prawns. It is cooked as a whole omelette and then sliced for serving as part of a Chinese meal.

Nutritional Information
Calories 309
Protein 34g
Carbohydrate 0.2g
Sugars 0g
Fat 19g
Saturates 5g

INGREDIENTS

8 eggs

225 g/8 oz cooked chicken, shredded

12 raw tiger prawns, peeled and deveined

2 tbsp snipped fresh chives

2 tsp light soy sauce

dash of chilli sauce

2 tbsp vegetable oil

1 Lightly beat the eggs in a large bowl. Add the shredded chicken and tiger prawns and mix well.

2 Stir in the snipped chives, light soy sauce and chilli sauce, mixing well to blend the ingredients together.

3 Heat the oil in a large, heavy-based frying pan over a medium heat. Pour in the egg mixture, tilting the frying pan to coat the base evenly and completely.

4 Cook over a medium heat, gently stirring the omelette with a fork, until the surface is just set and the underside is a golden brown colour.

5 When the omelette is set, slide it out of the frying pan with a palette knife. Cut the omelette into squares or slices and serve immediately.

VARIATION
You could add extra flavour to the omelette by stirring in 3 tbsp of finely chopped fresh coriander or 1 tsp of sesame seeds with the snipped chives in Step 2.

serves 4

Old English
Spicy Chicken Salad

10 MINUTES TO COOK

For this simple, refreshing summer salad you can use leftover roast chicken or ready-roasted chicken to save time. Add the dressing just before serving or the spinach will lose its crispness.

Nutritional Information
Calories 225
Protein 25g
Carbohydrate 4g
Sugars 4g
Fat 12g
Saturates 2g

INGREDIENTS

250 g/9 oz young spinach leaves

3 celery sticks

½ cucumber

2 spring onions

3 tbsp chopped fresh parsley

350 g/12 oz boneless, roast chicken, thinly sliced

smoked almonds, to garnish (optional)

DRESSING

2.5-cm/1-inch piece fresh root ginger, finely grated

3 tbsp olive oil

1 tbsp white wine vinegar

1 tbsp clear honey

½ tsp ground cinnamon

salt and pepper

1 Thoroughly wash the spinach leaves under cold running water, then pat dry with kitchen paper.

2 Using a sharp knife, thinly slice the celery, cucumber and spring onions. Toss in a large bowl with the spinach leaves and parsley. Transfer to serving plates and arrange the chicken on top of the salad.

3 Mix all the dressing ingredients together in a screw-topped jar and shake well. Season the dressing to taste with salt and pepper, then pour over the salad just before serving. Sprinkle with a few smoked almonds (if using).

2

2

3

10 MINUTES TO COOK Fruity Coleslaw

Most ready-made coleslaw seems to be smothered in a mayonnaise. You will notice the difference when you taste this colourful version, made with raw cabbage and fruit.

Nutritional Information
Calories 234
Protein 3g
Carbohydrate 30g
Sugars 30g
Fat 12g
Saturates 2g

INGREDIENTS

½ small red cabbage, thinly shredded
½ small white cabbage, thinly shredded
175 g/6 oz dried dates, stoned and chopped
1 red eating apple
2 green eating apples
4 tbsp lemon juice
25 g/1 oz pine kernels, toasted

DRESSING
5 tbsp olive oil
2 tbsp cider vinegar
1 tsp clear honey
salt and pepper

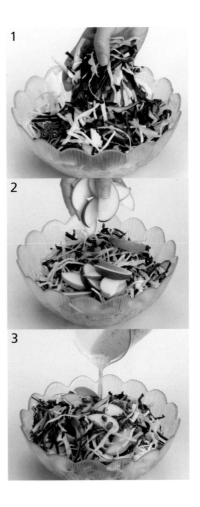

1 Place the red and white cabbage in a large salad bowl with the dates and toss well to mix.

2 Core the apples, but do not peel them. Thinly slice and place in a separate bowl. Add the lemon juice and toss well to prevent discoloration. Add them to the salad bowl.

3 To make the dressing, whisk the oil, vinegar and honey together in a small bowl and season to taste with salt and pepper. Pour the dressing over the salad and toss. Sprinkle with the pine kernels, toss lightly and serve.

COOK'S TIP
A good way to mix salad dressings is to place all the ingredients in a screw-top jar, put on the lid and shake vigorously to combine.

Mozzarella & Tomatoes

10 MINUTES TO COOK

Known as insalata tricolore *in Italy, this attractive and tasty starter deserves the best ingredients. Try to obtain* mozzarella di bufala, *the genuine cheese made from water buffalo milk.*

Nutritional Information
Calories 446
Protein 20g
Carbohydrate 5g
Sugars 5g
Fat 39g
Saturates 13g

INGREDIENTS

600 g/1 lb 5 oz tomatoes

300 g/10½ oz mozzarella cheese

16 fresh basil leaves, torn if large

125 ml/4 fl oz extra virgin olive oil, to serve

1 Using a sharp knife, cut the tomatoes into even slices about 5 mm/¼ inch thick. Drain the mozzarella cheese and discard the whey. Slice the mozzarella cheese evenly.

2 Arrange the tomato and mozzarella slices, overlapping slightly, in concentric circles on a large serving plate.

3 Sprinkle the basil over the salad and serve immediately with the oil for drizzling.

COOK'S TIP
If you can find them, use fresh plum tomatoes as they are less watery than the standard round varieties. Try to use sun-ripened tomatoes as they have a richer flavour.

10 MINUTES TO COOK Italian Platter

This popular hors d'oeuvre usually consists of vegetables soaked in olive oil and rich, creamy cheeses. Try this great low-fat version.

Nutritional Information
Calories 198
Protein 12g
Carbohydrate 25g
Sugars 12g
Fat 6g
Saturates 3g

INGREDIENTS

125 g/4½ oz reduced-fat
mozzarella cheese, drained
55 g/2 oz lean Parma ham
400 g/14 oz canned artichoke hearts,
drained
4 ripe figs
1 small mango
few plain grissini (breadsticks),
to serve
DRESSING
1 small orange
1 tbsp passata
1 tsp wholegrain mustard
4 tbsp low-fat natural yogurt
salt and pepper
fresh basil leaves

1 Cut the cheese into 12 sticks, 6 cm/2½ inches long. Remove the fat from the ham and slice the meat into 12 strips. Carefully wrap a strip of ham around each stick of cheese and arrange neatly on a serving platter.

2 Halve the artichoke hearts and cut the figs into quarters. Arrange them on the serving platter in groups.

3 Peel the mango, then slice it down each side of the large, flat central stone. Slice the flesh into strips and arrange them so that they form a fan shape on the serving platter.

4 To make the dressing, pare the rind from half of the orange using a vegetable peeler. Cut the rind into small strips and place them in a bowl. Squeeze the juice from the orange and add it to the bowl containing the rind.

5 Add the passata, mustard, yogurt and salt and pepper to the bowl and mix together. Shred the basil leaves and mix them into the dressing.

6 Spoon the dressing into a small dish and serve with the Italian Platter, accompanied by breadsticks.

VARIATION
For a change, serve with a French baguette or an Italian bread, widely available from supermarkets, and use to mop up the delicious dressing.

Lamb's Lettuce & Beetroot Salad

10 MINUTES TO COOK

This mouthwatering side salad has a subtle flavour that will not overpower the main dish. It will also add a splash of colour to any dinner table.

Nutritional Information
Calories 339
Protein 3g
Carbohydrate 7g
Sugars 7g
Fat 33g
Saturates 7g

INGREDIENTS

175 g/6 oz lamb's lettuce

4 small beetroot, cooked and diced

2 tbsp chopped walnuts

DRESSING

2 tbsp lemon juice

2 garlic cloves, finely chopped

1 tbsp Dijon mustard

pinch of sugar

salt and pepper

125 ml/4 fl oz sunflower oil

125 ml/4 fl oz soured cream

1

2

3

1 To make the dressing, place the lemon juice, garlic, mustard and sugar in a bowl, mix well, then season to taste with salt and pepper. Gradually whisk in the oil. Lightly beat the soured cream, then whisk it into the dressing.

2 Place the lamb's lettuce in a large bowl and pour over one-third of the dressing. Toss to coat.

3 Divide the lettuce between 4 serving bowls. Top each portion with beetroot and drizzle the remaining dressing over them. Sprinkle with chopped walnuts and serve.

10 MINUTES TO COOK

Chef's Salad

The name of the chef responsible for this substantial salad with its piquant Thousand Island dressing seems to be lost in the mists of time – but he was clearly a good chap.

Nutritional Information
Calories 730
Protein 41g
Carbohydrate 5g
Sugars 5g
Fat 61g
Saturates 15g

INGREDIENTS

1 iceberg lettuce, shredded

175 g/6 oz cooked ham, cut into thin strips

175 g/6 oz cooked tongue, cut into thin strips

350 g/12 oz cooked chicken, cut into thin strips

175 g/6 oz Gruyère cheese

4 tomatoes, quartered

3 hard-boiled eggs, shelled and quartered

400 ml/14 fl oz Thousand Island dressing

1 Arrange the lettuce on a large serving platter. Arrange the cold meat decoratively on top.

2 Cut the Gruyère cheese into batons.

3 Arrange the cheese batons over the salad, and the tomato and egg quarters around the edge of the platter. Serve the salad immediately, handing round the dressing separately.

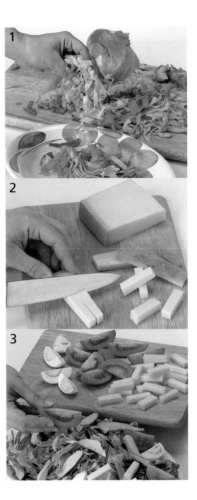

COOK'S TIP
This is a good salad to take on a picnic. Pack the salad in a large rigid container and store the dressing in a separate covered bowl, then serve the salad and dressing separately.

10 mins

 5 mins

serves 4

20 MINUTES TO COOK

Coconut & Crab Soup

Thai red curry paste is quite fiery, but adds a superb flavour to this soup. It is available in jars or packets from most supermarkets.

Nutritional Information
Calories 122
Protein 11g
Carbohydrate 11g
Sugars 9g
Fat 4g
Saturates 1g

INGREDIENTS

1 tbsp groundnut oil
2 tbsp Thai red curry paste
1 red pepper, halved, deseeded and sliced
600 ml/1 pint coconut milk
600 ml/1 pint fish stock
2 tbsp Thai fish sauce
225 g/8 oz canned or fresh white crabmeat
225 g/8 oz fresh or frozen crab claws
2 tbsp chopped fresh coriander
3 spring onions, sliced

1 Heat the oil in a preheated wok or large, heavy-based saucepan, swirling it around to coat. Add the curry paste and red pepper and stir-fry over a medium heat for 1 minute.

2 Add the coconut milk, fish stock and fish sauce and bring to the boil.

3 Add the crabmeat, crab claws, fresh coriander and spring onions.

4 Stir the mixture well and heat thoroughly for 2–3 minutes, or until the soup is warmed through.

5 Transfer to warmed soup bowls and serve hot.

COOK'S TIP
Clean the wok after use by washing it with water, using a mild detergent if necessary, and a cloth or brush. Dry thoroughly, then wipe the surface all over with a little oil to protect it.

64

20 MINUTES TO COOK Chicken & Herb Fritters

These fritters are delicious served with a green salad, a fresh vegetable salsa or a chilli sauce dip.

Nutritional Information
Calories 333
Protein 16g
Carbohydrate 17g
Sugars 1g
Fat 23g
Saturates 5g

INGREDIENTS

**500 g/1 lb 2 oz mashed potatoes,
  with butter added**

250 g/9 oz cooked chicken, chopped

125 g/4½ oz cooked ham, finely chopped

1 tbsp dried mixed herbs

2 eggs, lightly beaten

salt and pepper

milk

125 g/4½ oz fresh brown breadcrumbs

sunflower oil, for shallow-frying

fresh parsley sprigs, to garnish

mixed salad, to serve

1 Blend the mashed potatoes, chicken, ham, herbs and 1 beaten egg together in a large bowl. Season well with salt and pepper.

2 Shape the mixture into flat patties or small balls. Add a little milk to the second beaten egg.

3 Place the breadcrumbs on a plate. Dip the patties in the egg and milk mixture, then roll in the breadcrumbs to coat them completely.

4 Heat the oil in a large frying pan and cook the fritters until they are golden brown. Garnish with a fresh parsley sprig and serve with a mixed salad.

COOK'S TIP
Serve the fritters with a tomato sauce: heat 200 ml/7 fl oz passata and 4 tablespoons dry white wine. Season, remove from the heat and add 4 tablespoons natural yogurt. Reheat and add chilli powder to taste.

Mango Salad

This is an unusual combination but works well as long as the mango is very unripe. Pawpaw can be used instead, if you prefer.

Nutritional Information
Calories 26
Protein 1g
Carbohydrate 6g
Sugars 3g
Fat 0.2g
Saturates 0g

INGREDIENTS

6 roasted canned chestnuts, quartered

1 small fresh red chilli, deseeded and finely chopped

2 shallots, finely chopped

2 tbsp lemon juice

1 tbsp light soy sauce

1 large unripe mango, peeled and cut into long thin shreds

1 watermelon

1 lollo biondo lettuce, or any crunchy lettuce

15 g/½ oz fresh coriander leaves

1 Soak the mango briefly in cold water to remove any syrup. Mix the chilli, shallots, lemon juice and soy sauce together in a small bowl. Drain the mango and mix with the chestnuts together in a separate bowl.

2 To make the melon basket, stand the watermelon on one end on a level surface. Holding a knife level and in one place, turn the watermelon on its axis so that the knife marks an even line all around the centre. Mark a 2.5 cm/1 inch wide handle across the top and through the centre stem, joining the middle line at either end.

3 Take a sharp knife and, following the marks made for the handle, make the first vertical cut. Then cut down the other side of the handle. Now follow the middle line and make your straight or zigzag cut, taking care that the knife is always pointing towards the centre of the watermelon and is level with the work surface, as this ensures that when you reach the handle cuts, the cut out piece of melon will pull away cleanly.

4 Hollow out the flesh with a spoon, leaving a clean edge. Line the melon basket with the lettuce and coriander. Fill with the mango mixture, pour over the dressing and serve immediately.

20 MINUTES TO COOK

Broad Beans with Feta

This simple dish captures the heady flavours of the Greek islands and can be served as a salad or as a hot or cold appetizer.

Nutritional Information
Calories 140
Protein 6g
Carbohydrate 6g
Sugars 1g
Fat 10g
Saturates 3g

INGREDIENTS

500 g/1 lb 2 oz shelled broad beans

4 tbsp extra virgin olive oil

1 tbsp lemon juice

salt and pepper

1 tbsp finely chopped fresh dill,
   plus extra to garnish

55 g/2 oz feta cheese, drained and diced

lemon wedges, to serve

1 Bring a saucepan of water to the boil. Add the broad beans and cook for 2 minutes, until tender. Drain thoroughly and reserve.

2 When the beans are cool enough to handle, remove and discard the outer skins to reveal the bright green beans underneath (see Cook's Tip). Place the peeled beans in a serving bowl.

3 Mix the oil and lemon juice together in a bowl, then season to taste with salt and pepper. Pour the dressing over the warm beans, add the dill and stir gently. Taste and adjust the seasoning, if necessary.

4 If serving hot, add the feta cheese, toss gently and sprinkle with extra dill, then serve immediately. Alternatively, leave the beans in their dressing to cool, then chill until required.

5 To serve cold, remove from the refrigerator 10 minutes before serving to bring to room temperature. Taste and adjust the seasoning, if necessary, then sprinkle with the feta and extra dill. Serve with lemon wedges.

COOK'S TIP
If you are lucky enough to have very young broad beans at the start of the season, it isn't necessary to remove the outer skin.

20 MINUTES TO COOK

Greek Salad

The combination of juicy, ripe tomatoes and black olives is a classic partnership, but Greek cooks also add feta cheese for a salty flavour.

Nutritional Information
Calories 347
Protein 12g
Carbohydrate 6g
Sugars 6g
Fat 31g
Saturates 11g

INGREDIENTS

250 g/9 oz feta cheese

250 g/9 oz cucumber

250 g/9 oz Greek kalamata olives

1 red onion or 4 spring onions

2 large juicy tomatoes

1 tsp clear honey

4 tbsp extra virgin olive oil

½ lemon

salt and pepper

fresh or dried oregano, to garnish

pitta bread, to serve

1 Drain the feta cheese if it is packed in brine. Place it on a chopping board and cut into 1-cm/½-inch dice. Transfer to a salad bowl.

2 Cut the cucumber in half lengthways and use a teaspoon to scoop out the seeds. Cut the flesh into 1-cm/½-inch slices and add to the bowl.

3 Stone the olives, if preferred, and add them to the salad bowl. Slice the red onion or finely chop the spring onions and add to the salad bowl. Cut each tomato into quarters and scoop out the seeds with a teaspoon. Cut the flesh into bite-sized pieces and add to the bowl.

4 Using your hands, gently toss all the ingredients together. Stir the honey into the olive oil (see Cook's Tip), add to the salad and squeeze in lemon juice to taste. Season with pepper and a little salt, if wished. Cover with clingfilm and chill until required.

5 Garnish the salad with the oregano and serve with pitta bread.

COOK'S TIP
The small amount of honey helps to bring out the full flavour of the tomatoes.

72

20 MINUTES TO COOK

Capri Salad

This tomato, olive and mozzarella salad, dressed with balsamic vinegar and extra virgin olive oil, makes a delicious starter on its own.

Nutritional Information
Calories 95
Protein 3g
Carbohydrate 3g
Sugars 3g
Fat 8g
Saturates 3g

INGREDIENTS

2 beef tomatoes
125 g/4½ oz mozzarella cheese
12 black olives
8 fresh basil leaves
1 tbsp balsamic vinegar
1 tbsp extra virgin olive oil
salt and pepper
fresh basil leaves, to garnish

1 Preheat the grill to medium. Cut the tomatoes into thin slices.

2 Drain the mozzarella cheese, if necessary, and cut into thin slices with a sharp knife.

3 Stone the black olives, if necessary, and slice into rings.

4 Layer the tomatoes, mozzarella cheese slices, olives and basil leaves in a stack, finishing with a layer of mozzarella cheese on top.

5 Place the stacks under the hot grill for 2–3 minutes, or just long enough to melt the mozzarella.

6 Drizzle over the balsamic vinegar and oil and season to taste with a little salt and pepper.

7 Transfer to 4 large serving plates and garnish with a few fresh basil leaves. Serve immediately.

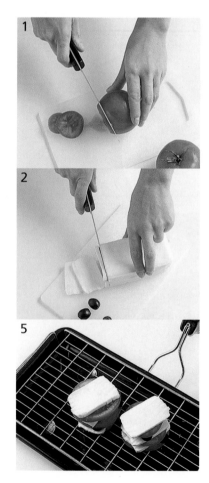

COOK'S TIP
Buffalo mozzarella cheese, although it is usually more expensive because of the comparative rarity of buffaloes, does have a better flavour than the cow's milk variety. It is popular in salads, but also provides a tangy layer in baked dishes.

Griddled Smoked Salmon

It is best to buy packets of smoked salmon slices for this recipe as they lend themselves to folding more easily than freshly sliced salmon.

Nutritional Information
Calories 115
Protein 23g
Carbohydrate 1g
Sugars 1g
Fat 15g
Saturates 2g

INGREDIENTS

350 g/12 oz sliced smoked salmon
1 tsp Dijon mustard
1 garlic clove, crushed
2 tsp chopped fresh dill
2 tsp sherry vinegar
salt and pepper
4 tbsp olive oil
115 g/4 oz mixed salad leaves
TO GARNISH
fresh dill sprigs
mixed lemon, lime and orange slices

1 Fold the slices of smoked salmon, making 2 folds accordion-style, so that they form little parcels.

2 To make the vinaigrette, whisk the mustard, garlic, dill, vinegar and salt and pepper together in a small bowl. Gradually whisk in the olive oil to form a light emulsion.

3 Heat a ridged griddle pan over a medium heat until smoking. Add the salmon parcels and cook on one side only for 2–3 minutes, until heated through and marked from the pan.

4 Meanwhile, dress the salad leaves with some of the vinaigrette and divide between 4 serving plates. Top with the cooked smoked salmon, cooked side up. Drizzle with the remaining dressing. Garnish with a few sprigs of fresh dill and a mixture of lemon, lime and orange slices. Serve.

1   2   3

20 MINUTES TO COOK Fettuccine all'Alfredo

This simple, traditional dish can be made with any long pasta, but is especially good with flat noodles, such as fettuccine or tagliatelle.

Nutritional Information
Calories 627
Protein 18g
Carbohydrate 51g
Sugars 2g
Fat 41g
Saturates 23g

INGREDIENTS

25 g/1 oz butter
200 ml/7 fl oz double cream
salt and pepper
450 g/1 lb fresh fettuccine
85 g/3 oz freshly grated Parmesan cheese, plus extra to serve
pinch of freshly grated nutmeg
1 fresh flat-leaved parsley sprig, to garnish

1 Place the butter and 150 ml/5 fl oz of the cream into a large saucepan and bring to the boil over a medium heat. Reduce the heat, then simmer gently for 1½ minutes, or until the sauce has thickened slightly.

2 Meanwhile, bring a large saucepan of lightly salted water to the boil. Add the pasta, return to the boil and cook for 2–3 minutes, or until tender but still firm to the bite. Drain the pasta thoroughly, then pour over the cream sauce.

3 Toss the pasta in the sauce over a low heat until coated thoroughly.

4 Add the remaining cream, the Parmesan cheese and nutmeg to the pasta mixture, then season to taste with plenty of salt and pepper. Toss thoroughly to coat the pasta while gently heating through.

5 Transfer the pasta mixture to a large, warmed serving dish and garnish with a parsley sprig. Serve immediately with extra Parmesan cheese, if you wish.

VARIATION
This classic Roman dish is often served with the addition of strips of ham and fresh peas. Add 225 g/8 oz shelled cooked peas and 175 g/6 oz ham strips with the Parmesan cheese in Step 4.

20 MINUTES TO COOK

Chinese Chicken

As in all Chinese dishes, the matching and contrasting flavours, colours and textures in this recipe produce a harmonious – and delicious – result.

Nutritional Information
Calories 214
Protein 18g
Carbohydrate 4g
Sugars 2g
Fat 14g
Saturates 3g

INGREDIENTS

280 g/10 oz skinless, boneless chicken breast, very thinly sliced

¼ tsp cornflour

1¼ tsp water

1 small egg white, lightly beaten

salt

4 tbsp groundnut oil

2 spring onions, cut into short lengths

115 g/4 oz green beans, halved

8 shiitake mushrooms, halved if large

115 g/4 oz canned bamboo shoots, drained and rinsed

1 tsp finely chopped fresh root ginger

1 tbsp dark soy sauce

1 tbsp rice wine or dry sherry

1 tsp light brown sugar

dash of sesame oil

freshly cooked rice, to serve

1 Cut the chicken slices into small pieces and place in a bowl. Mix the cornflour and water together until a smooth paste forms and add to the chicken with the egg white and a pinch of salt. Stir well to coat.

2 Heat the groundnut oil in a preheated wok or large, heavy-based frying pan. Add the chicken and stir-fry over a medium heat for 45 seconds, or until browned. Remove from the wok with a slotted spoon.

3 Increase the heat to high, add the spring onions, green beans, mushrooms, bamboo shoots and ginger and stir-fry for 1 minute. Return the chicken to the wok. Mix the soy sauce and rice wine together in a small jug and add to the wok with the sugar and a pinch of salt. Cook, stirring constantly, for a further 1 minute. Sprinkle with a dash of sesame oil and serve immediately with rice.

COOK'S TIP
Try serving this stir-fry with rice sticks. These are broad, pale, translucent ribbon noodles made from ground rice.

2

Chicken Fu Yung

20 MINUTES TO COOK

Although commonly described as an omelette, for a more authentic fu yung you should use only egg whites – it creates a very delicate texture.

Nutritional Information
Calories 220
Protein 16g
Carbohydrate 7g
Sugars 1g
Fat 14g
Saturates 3g

INGREDIENTS

175 g/6 oz chicken breast fillet, skinned
salt and pepper
1 tsp rice wine or dry sherry
1 tbsp cornflour
3 eggs
½ tsp spring onions, finely chopped
3 tbsp vegetable oil
125 g/4½ oz green peas
1 tsp light soy sauce
drops of sesame oil

1 Cut the chicken across the grain into very small, paper-thin slices, using a cleaver. Place the chicken slices in a shallow dish.

2 Mix ½ teaspoon salt, the pepper, rice wine and cornflour together in a small bowl.

3 Pour the mixture over the chicken slices in the dish, turning the chicken until well coated.

4 Beat the eggs in a small bowl with a pinch of salt and the spring onions.

5 Heat the vegetable oil in a preheated wok. Add the chicken slices and stir-fry for 1 minute, making sure that the slices are kept separated.

6 Pour the beaten eggs over the chicken, and lightly scramble until set. Do not stir too vigorously, or the mixture will break up in the oil. Stir the oil from the base of the wok so that the fu yung rises to the surface.

7 Add the peas, light soy sauce and salt to taste and blend well. Transfer the fu yung to warmed serving dishes, sprinkle with sesame oil and serve.

COOK'S TIP
If available, chicken goujons can be used for this dish: these are small, delicate strips of chicken which require no further cutting and are very tender.

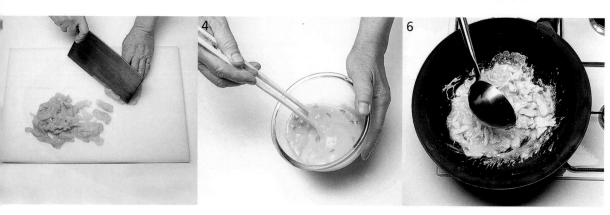

4

6

20 MINUTES TO COOK

Spicy Peanut Chicken

This quick dish has many variations, but this version includes the classic combination of peanuts, chicken and chillies.

Nutritional Information
Calories 342
Protein 25g
Carbohydrate 6g
Sugars 3g
Fat 24g
Saturates 5g

INGREDIENTS

2 tbsp groundnut oil

125 g/4½ oz shelled peanuts

300 g/10½ oz skinless, boneless chicken breast, cut into 2.5-cm/1-inch cubes

1 fresh red chilli, sliced

1 green pepper, deseeded and cut into strips

SAUCE

150 ml/5 fl oz chicken stock

1 tbsp rice wine or dry sherry

1 tbsp light soy sauce

1½ tsp light brown sugar

2 garlic cloves, crushed

1 tsp grated fresh root ginger

1 tsp rice wine vinegar

1 tsp sesame oil

1 Heat the groundnut oil in a preheated wok or large, heavy-based frying pan.

2 Add the peanuts to the wok and stir-fry for 1 minute. Remove the peanuts with a slotted spoon and reserve.

3 Add the chicken to the wok and cook for 1–2 minutes.

4 Stir in the chilli and green pepper and cook for 1 minute. Remove the chicken, chilli and green pepper from the wok with a slotted spoon and reserve until required.

5 Place half of the peanuts in a food processor and process until almost smooth. If necessary, add a little stock to form a smoother paste. Alternatively, place them in a plastic bag and crush with a rolling pin.

6 To make the sauce, add the chicken stock, rice wine, light soy sauce, light brown sugar, garlic, ginger and rice wine vinegar to the wok.

7 Heat the sauce without boiling and stir in the peanut paste, the remaining peanuts and the chicken mixture. Mix well until all the ingredients are thoroughly blended.

8 Sprinkle the sesame oil into the wok, stir and cook for 1 minute. Transfer the chicken to a warmed serving dish and serve immediately.

5

7

20 MINUTES TO COOK Celery & Cashew Chicken

Stir-fry yellow bean sauce gives this quick and easy Chinese dish a really authentic taste. Pecan nuts can be used in place of the cashews.

Nutritional Information
Calories 549
Protein 41g
Carbohydrate 28g
Sugars 24g
Fat 31g
Saturates 5g

INGREDIENTS

3–4 skinless, boneless chicken breasts, about 625 g/1 lb 6 oz
2 tbsp sunflower or vegetable oil
125 g/4½ oz cashew nuts
4–6 spring onions, thinly sliced diagonally
5–6 celery sticks, thinly sliced diagonally
1 x 175 g/6 oz jar stir-fry yellow bean sauce
salt and pepper
freshly cooked rice, to serve
celery leaves, to garnish (optional)

1 Using a sharp knife or metal cleaver, cut the chicken into thin slices across the grain.

2 Heat the oil in a preheated wok or large frying pan, swirling it around until it is really hot.

3 Add the cashew nuts and stir-fry until they begin to brown but do not allow them to burn.

4 Add the chicken and stir-fry until well sealed and almost cooked through.

5 Add the spring onions and celery and continue to stir-fry for 2–3 minutes, stirring the food well around the wok.

6 Add the yellow bean sauce to the wok and season lightly with salt and pepper.

7 Toss the mixture in the wok until the chicken and vegetables are thoroughly coated with the sauce and piping hot.

8 Serve immediately with rice, garnished with celery leaves, if liked.

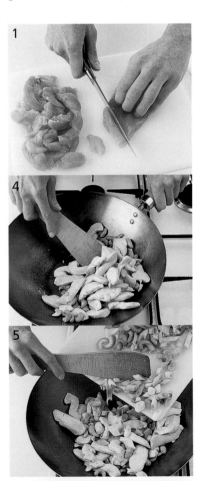

VARIATION
This recipe can be adapted to use turkey fillets or steaks, or pork fillet or boneless steaks. Cut the turkey or pork lengthways first, then slice thinly across the grain.

20 MINUTES TO COOK   Veal Chops with Salsa Verde

*This vibrant green Italian sauce adds
a touch of Mediterranean flavour
to any simply cooked meat or seafood.*

Nutritional Information

Calories 481

Protein 41g

Carbohydrate 2g

Sugars 1g

Fat 34g

Saturates 5g

INGREDIENTS

**4 veal chops, such as loin chops, about
225 g/8 oz each and 2 cm/¾ inch thick**

garlic-flavoured olive oil, for brushing

salt and pepper

fresh basil or oregano leaves, to garnish

SALSA VERDE

55 g/2 oz fresh flat-leaved parsley leaves

3 canned anchovy fillets in oil, drained

1½ tsp capers in brine, rinsed and drained

1 shallot, finely chopped

**1 garlic clove, halved, green core removed,
and chopped**

1 tbsp lemon juice

**6 large fresh basil leaves or ¾ tsp
freeze-dried basil**

2 fresh oregano sprigs or ½ tsp dried oregano

125 ml/4 fl oz extra virgin olive oil

1 Preheat the grill to medium. To make
the salsa verde, place the parsley,
anchovies, capers, shallot, garlic, lemon
juice, basil and oregano in a food
processor or blender and process until
thoroughly chopped and blended.

2 With the motor running, add the oil
through the feeder tube or top and
process until thickened. Season with
pepper to taste. Scrape to a bowl,
cover with clingfilm and leave to chill in
the refrigerator.

3 Lightly brush the veal chops with the
oil and season to taste with salt and
pepper. Place under the hot grill and
cook for 3 minutes. Turn over, brush
with more oil and grill for a further
2 minutes, or until cooked when tested
with the tip of a knife.

4 Transfer the chops to 4 warmed
serving plates and spoon a little of the
chilled salsa verde beside them. Garnish
the chops with fresh basil and serve
with the remaining salsa verde
handed separately.

20 MINUTES TO COOK Lamb with Noodles

Lamb is quick-fried, coated in a soy sauce and served on a bed of transparent noodles for a richly flavoured dish.

Nutritional Information
Calories 285
Protein 27g
Carbohydrate 10g
Sugars 1g
Fat 16g
Saturates 6g

INGREDIENTS

150 g/5½ oz cellophane noodles

2 tbsp groundnut oil

450 g/1 lb lean lamb, thinly sliced

2 garlic cloves, crushed

2 leeks, sliced

3 tbsp dark soy sauce

250 ml/9 fl oz lamb stock

dash of chilli sauce

fresh red chilli strips, to garnish

1 Bring a large saucepan of water to the boil. Add the cellophane noodles and cook for 1 minute. Drain the noodles well, place in a sieve, rinse under cold running water and drain thoroughly again. Reserve until required.

2 Heat the groundnut oil in a preheated wok or frying pan, swirling the oil around until it is really hot.

3 Add the lamb to the wok and stir-fry for 2 minutes.

4 Add the crushed garlic and sliced leeks to the wok and stir-fry for a further 2 minutes.

5 Stir in the dark soy sauce, lamb stock and chilli sauce and cook for 3–4 minutes, stirring frequently, until the meat is cooked through.

6 Add the drained cellophane noodles to the wok and cook for 1 minute, stirring constantly, until heated through.

7 Transfer the lamb and cellophane noodles to serving plates, garnish with red chilli strips and serve.

COOK'S TIP
Transparent noodles are usually available in Chinese supermarkets. If unavailable, use egg noodles instead, and cook them according to the instructions on the packet.

20 MINUTES TO COOK

Lamb with Mushroom Sauce

Use a lean cut of lamb, such as fillet, for this recipe for both flavour and tenderness.

Nutritional Information
Calories 219
Protein 21g
Carbohydrate 4g
Sugars 1g
Fat 14g
Saturates 4g

INGREDIENTS

350 g/12 oz lean boneless lamb, such as fillet or loin
2 tbsp vegetable oil
3 garlic cloves, crushed
1 leek, sliced
175 g/6 oz large mushrooms, sliced
½ tsp sesame oil
fresh red chillies, to garnish

SAUCE

1 tsp cornflour
4 tbsp light soy sauce
3 tbsp rice wine or dry sherry
3 tbsp water
½ tsp chilli sauce

1 Using a sharp knife or meat cleaver, cut the lamb into thin strips.

2 Heat the vegetable oil in a preheated wok or large frying pan.

3 Add the lamb strips, garlic and leek and stir-fry for 2–3 minutes.

4 To make the sauce, mix the cornflour, soy sauce, rice wine, water and chilli sauce together in a bowl and reserve until required.

5 Add the sliced mushrooms to the wok and stir-fry for 1 minute. Stir in the prepared sauce and cook for 2–3 minutes, or until the lamb is cooked through and tender.

6 Sprinkle the sesame oil over the top and transfer the lamb and mushrooms to a warmed serving dish. Garnish with red chillies and serve immediately.

VARIATION
The lamb can be replaced with lean steak or pork fillet in this classic recipe from Beijing. You could also use 2–3 spring onions, 1 shallot or 1 small onion instead of the leek, if you prefer.

20 MINUTES TO COOK

Sesame Lamb Stir-fry

This is a very simple, yet delicious dish, in which lean pieces of lamb are cooked in a sweet soy sauce and then sprinkled with sesame seeds.

Nutritional Information
Calories 276
Protein 25g
Carbohydrate 5g
Sugars 4g
Fat 18g
Saturates 6g

INGREDIENTS

2 tbsp groundnut oil

450 g/1 lb boneless lean lamb,
   cut into thin strips

2 leeks, sliced

1 carrot, cut into matchsticks

2 garlic cloves, crushed

85 ml/3 fl oz lamb or vegetable stock

2 tsp light brown sugar

1 tbsp dark soy sauce

4½ tsp sesame seeds

1 Heat the groundnut oil in a preheated wok or large, heavy-based frying pan until it is very hot.

2 Add the lamb and stir-fry for 2–3 minutes. Remove the lamb from the wok with a slotted spoon and reserve until required.

3 Add the leeks, carrot and garlic to the wok and stir-fry for 1–2 minutes.

4 Remove the vegetables from the wok with a slotted spoon and reserve.

5 Drain any remaining oil from the wok. Place the stock, light brown sugar and dark soy sauce in the wok and add the lamb. Cook, stirring constantly for 2–3 minutes, until the lamb is coated in the mixture.

6 Sprinkle the sesame seeds over the top, turning the lamb to coat.

7 Spoon the leek, carrot and garlic mixture into a warmed serving dish and top with the lamb. Serve immediately.

COOK'S TIP
Be careful not to burn the sugar in the wok when coating the meat, otherwise the flavour of the dish will be spoiled.

94

20 MINUTES TO COOK Peppered Beef Cashew

A simple but stunning dish of tender strips of beef mixed with crunchy cashew nuts, coated in a hot sauce. Serve with rice noodles.

Nutritional Information
Calories 403
Protein 26g
Carbohydrate 11g
Sugars 7g
Fat 29g
Saturates 9g

INGREDIENTS

1 tbsp groundnut or sunflower oil

1 tbsp sesame oil

1 onion, sliced

1 garlic clove, crushed

1 tbsp grated fresh root ginger

500 g/1 lb 2 oz fillet or rump steak, cut into thin strips

2 tsp palm sugar (see Cook's Tip)

2 tbsp light soy sauce

1 small yellow pepper, cored, deseeded and sliced

1 red pepper, cored, deseeded and sliced

4 spring onions, chopped

2 celery sticks, chopped

4 large open-cap mushrooms, sliced

4 tbsp roasted cashew nuts

3 tbsp stock or white wine

freshly cooked rice noodles, to serve

1 Heat the oils in a large, heavy-based frying pan or wok. Add the onion, garlic and ginger and stir-fry for 2 minutes, until softened.

2 Add the steak strips and stir-fry for a further 2–3 minutes, or until the meat has browned.

3 Add the sugar and soy sauce, stirring to mix well.

4 Add the peppers, spring onions, celery, mushrooms and cashew nuts, mixing well.

5 Add the stock or white wine and stir-fry for 2–3 minutes, until the beef is cooked through and the vegetables are tender-crisp.

6 Serve the stir-fry immediately with freshly cooked rice noodles.

COOK'S TIP
Palm sugar is a thick brown sugar with a slightly caramel taste. It is sold in cakes, or in small containers. If not available, use soft dark brown or demerara sugar instead.

20 MINUTES TO COOK Pad Thai Noodles

The combination of ingredients in this classic noodle dish varies, depending on the cook, but it commonly contains a mixture of pork and prawns or other seafood.

Nutritional Information
Calories 477
Protein 26g
Carbohydrate 60g
Sugars 6g
Fat 14g
Saturates 3g

INGREDIENTS

250 g/9 oz rice stick noodles

3 tbsp groundnut oil

3 garlic cloves, finely chopped

125 g/4½ oz pork fillet, chopped
　　into 5-mm/¼-inch pieces

200 g/7 oz cooked peeled prawns

1 tbsp sugar

3 tbsp Thai fish sauce

1 tbsp tomato ketchup

1 tbsp lime juice

2 eggs, beaten

125 g/4½ oz beansprouts

TO GARNISH

1 tsp dried red chilli flakes

2 spring onions, thickly sliced

2 tbsp chopped fresh coriander

1 Place the rice noodles in a bowl, cover with hot water and leave to soak for 15 minutes, or according to the packet instructions. Drain well and reserve until required.

2 Heat the oil in a large frying pan. Add the garlic and fry over a high heat for 30 seconds. Add the pork and stir-fry for 2–3 minutes, until browned.

3 Stir in the prawns, then add the sugar, fish sauce, ketchup and lime juice and continue stir-frying for a further 30 seconds.

4 Stir in the eggs and stir-fry until lightly set. Stir in the reserved noodles, then add the beansprouts and stir-fry for a further 30 seconds. Transfer to a serving dish and sprinkle with chilli flakes, spring onions and coriander. Serve immediately.

20 MINUTES TO COOK

Pasta with Garlic & Broccoli

Broccoli coated in a garlic-flavoured cream sauce, served on fresh herb tagliatelle. Try sprinkling with toasted pine kernels to add an extra crunch.

Nutritional Information
Calories 538
Protein 23g
Carbohydrate 50g
Sugars 4g
Fat 29g
Saturates 17g

INGREDIENTS

500 g/1 lb 2 oz broccoli
salt
300 g/10½ oz garlic and herb cream cheese
4 tbsp milk
350 g/12 oz fresh herb tagliatelle
25 g/1 oz freshly grated Parmesan cheese
snipped fresh chives, to garnish

1 Cut the broccoli into even-sized florets. Bring a saucepan of lightly salted water to the boil. Add the broccoli, return to the boil and cook for 3 minutes, then drain thoroughly. Reserve until required.

2 Place the soft cheese in a saucepan and heat over a low heat, stirring constantly, until melted. Add the milk and stir until well blended.

3 Add the broccoli to the cheese mixture and stir until the broccoli is well coated.

4 Meanwhile, bring a large saucepan of lightly salted water to the boil. Add the pasta, return to the boil and cook for 4–5 minutes, or until tender but still firm to the bite.

5 Drain the pasta thoroughly and transfer to 4 warmed serving plates. Spoon the broccoli and cheese sauce on top. Sprinkle with grated Parmesan cheese, garnish with snipped chives and serve immediately.

COOK'S TIP
A herb-flavoured pasta goes particularly well with the broccoli sauce, but failing this, a tagliatelle verde or *paglia e fieno* (literally 'straw and hay' – thin green and yellow noodles) will fit the bill.

Spaghetti with Smoked Salmon

serves 4

This luxurious dish is made in moments, and can be used to astonish and delight any unexpected guests.

Nutritional Information

Calories 949

Protein 26g

Carbohydrate 86g

Sugars 6g

Fat 49g

Saturates 27g

INGREDIENTS

450 g/1 lb dried white or buckwheat spaghetti

2 tbsp olive oil

SAUCE

300 ml/10 fl oz double cream

150 ml/5 fl oz whisky or brandy

125 g/4½ oz smoked salmon

pinch of cayenne pepper

black pepper

2 tbsp chopped fresh coriander or parsley

TO GARNISH

90 g/3¼ oz feta cheese, well drained and crumbled

fresh coriander or parsley sprigs

1 To cook the pasta, bring a large saucepan of lightly salted water to the boil. Add the pasta and half of the oil, return to the boil and cook until tender but still firm to the bite. Drain the pasta, return to the saucepan and sprinkle over the remaining oil. Cover, shake the saucepan and keep warm.

2 To make the sauce, pour the cream into a small saucepan and bring to simmering point, but do not let it boil. Pour the whisky into another small saucepan and bring to simmering point, but do not let it boil. Remove both saucepans from the heat and mix the cream with the whisky.

3 Cut the smoked salmon into thin strips and add to the cream sauce. Season to taste with cayenne and black pepper. Just before serving, stir in the chopped coriander.

4 Transfer the spaghetti to a warmed serving dish, pour over the sauce and toss thoroughly with 2 large forks. To garnish, sprinkle over the crumbled feta cheese and fresh coriander sprigs, then serve immediately.

Coconut Prawns

Fan-tail prawns give a special touch to a meal, especially when cooked in this delicious, crisp coconut coating.

Nutritional Information
Calories 236
Protein 27g
Carbohydrate 3g
Sugars 1g
Fat 13g
Saturates 7g

INGREDIENTS

50 g/1¾ oz desiccated coconut
25 g/1 oz fresh white breadcrumbs
1 tsp Chinese five-spice powder
½ tsp salt
finely grated rind of 1 lime
1 egg white
450 g/1 lb raw fan-tail prawns
sunflower or corn oil, for frying
lemon wedges, to garnish
soy or chilli sauce, to serve

1 Mix the desiccated coconut, white breadcrumbs, Chinese five-spice powder, salt and finely grated lime rind together in a bowl.

2 Lightly whisk the egg white in a separate bowl.

3 Rinse the prawns under cold running water and pat dry with kitchen paper.

4 Dip the prawns into the egg white, then into the coconut and breadcrumb mixture, so that they are evenly coated.

5 Heat about 5-cm/2-inches of sunflower oil in a preheated wok or large, heavy-based frying pan.

6 Add the prawns to the wok and stir-fry for 5 minutes, or until golden and crispy. Remove the prawns with a slotted spoon and leave to drain on kitchen paper.

7 Transfer the coconut prawns to warmed serving dishes and garnish with lemon wedges. Serve immediately with soy or chilli sauce.

COOK'S TIP
Chinese five-spice powder will keep for a few months if stored in a cool, dark place in an airtight container.

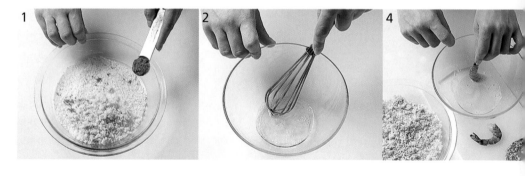

20 MINUTES TO COOK

Tuna & Vegetable Stir-fry

Fresh tuna is a dark, meaty fish and is now widely available at fresh fish counters. It lends itself perfectly to the rich flavours in this recipe.

Nutritional Information
Calories 245
Protein 30g
Carbohydrate 14g
Sugars 11g
Fat 7g
Saturates 1g

INGREDIENTS

225 g/8 oz carrots

2 tbsp sunflower or corn oil

1 onion, thinly sliced

175 g/6 oz mangetout

175 g/6 oz baby corn cobs, halved lengthways

450 g/1 lb fresh tuna

2 tbsp Thai fish sauce

1 tbsp palm sugar

finely grated rind and juice of 1 orange

2 tbsp sherry

1 tsp cornflour

freshly cooked noodles, to serve

1 Shred the carrots finely. Heat the corn oil in a preheated wok or large, heavy-based frying pan.

2 Add the onion, carrots, mangetout and baby corn cobs to the wok and stir-fry for 5 minutes.

3 Slice the tuna and add it to the wok. Stir-fry for 2–3 minutes, or until the tuna turns opaque.

4 Mix the fish sauce, palm sugar, orange rind and juice, sherry and cornflour together in a small bowl.

5 Pour the mixture over the tuna and vegetables and cook for 2 minutes, or until the juices thicken. Serve the stir-fry with noodles.

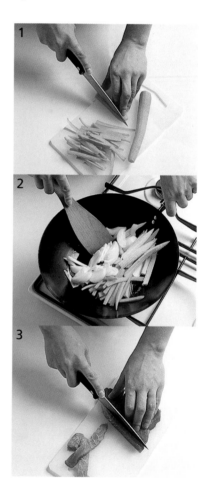

VARIATION
Try using swordfish steaks instead of the tuna. Swordfish steaks are now widely available and are similar in texture to tuna.

106

20 MINUTES TO COOK Giant Garlic Prawns

In Spain, giant garlic prawns are cooked in small half-glazed earthenware dishes called cazuelas. *The prawns arrive at your table sizzling.*

Nutritional Information
Calories 385
Protein 26g
Carbohydrate 1g
Sugars 0g
Fat 31g
Saturates 5g

INGREDIENTS

125 ml/4 fl oz olive oil

4 garlic cloves, finely chopped

2 hot fresh red chillies, deseeded and finely chopped

450 g/1 lb cooked king prawns

2 tbsp chopped fresh flat-leaved parsley

salt and pepper

lemon wedges, to garnish

crusty bread, to serve

1 Heat the olive oil in a large, heavy-based frying pan over a low heat. Add the garlic and chillies and cook, stirring occasionally, for 1–2 minutes, until softened but not coloured.

2 Add the prawns and stir-fry for 2–3 minutes, until heated through and coated in the oil and garlic mixture.

3 Turn off the heat and add the chopped parsley, stirring well to mix. Season to taste with salt and pepper.

4 Divide the prawns and garlic-flavoured oil between warmed serving dishes and garnish with lemon wedges. Serve with lots of crusty bread.

COOK'S TIP
If you can get hold of raw prawns, cook them as above but increase the cooking time to 5–6 minutes, until the prawns are cooked through and turn bright pink. If you are using frozen prawns, make sure they are thoroughly thawed before cooking.

Sesame Salmon with Cream

Salmon fillet holds its shape when tossed in sesame seeds and stir-fried. It is served in a delicious creamy sauce of diced courgettes.

Nutritional Information
Calories 550
Protein 35g
Carbohydrate 2g
Sugars 1g
Fat 45g
Saturates 12g

INGREDIENTS

625–750 g/1 lb 6 oz–1 lb 10 oz salmon or pink trout fillets

salt and pepper

2 tbsp light soy sauce

3 tbsp sesame seeds

3 tbsp sunflower oil

4 spring onions, thinly sliced diagonally

2 large courgettes, diced, or 12.5-cm/5-inch piece cucumber, diced

grated rind of ½ lemon

1 tbsp lemon juice

½ tsp ground turmeric

6 tbsp fish stock or water

3 tbsp double cream or fromage frais

curly endive, to garnish

1 Skin the fish and cut into strips about 4 x 2 cm/1½ x ¾ inch. Pat dry on kitchen paper. Season lightly with salt and pepper, then brush with soy sauce and sprinkle all over with sesame seeds.

2 Heat 2 tablespoons of oil in a preheated wok. Add the fish and stir-fry for 3–4 minutes, until lightly browned. Remove with a fish slice, drain on kitchen paper and keep warm.

3 Add the remaining oil to the wok and heat. Add the spring onions and courgettes and stir-fry for 1–2 minutes.

Add the lemon rind and juice, turmeric, stock and salt and pepper to taste and bring to the boil for 1 minute. Stir in the cream.

4 Return the fish to the wok and toss gently in the sauce until piping hot. Garnish with curly endive and serve.

20 MINUTES TO COOK

Noodles with Prawns

This is a simple dish using egg noodles and large prawns, which give the dish a wonderful flavour, texture and colour.

Nutritional Information
Calories 142
Protein 11g
Carbohydrate 11g
Sugars 0.4g
Fat 7g
Saturates 1g

INGREDIENTS

225 g/8 oz thin egg noodles

2 tbsp groundnut oil

1 garlic clove, crushed

½ tsp ground star anise

1 bunch of spring onions, cut into
   5-cm/2-inch pieces

24 raw tiger prawns, peeled with tails intact

2 tbsp light soy sauce

2 tsp lime juice

lime slices, to garnish

1 Bring a large saucepan of water to the boil. Add the noodles and cook for 2 minutes.

2 Drain the noodles well, rinse under cold running water and drain thoroughly again. Keep warm and reserve until required.

3 Heat a large wok over a high heat. Add the groundnut oil. When the oil is almost smoking, add the garlic and star anise and stir-fry for 30 seconds.

4 Add the spring onions and tiger prawns to the wok and stir-fry for 2–3 minutes.

5 Stir in the soy sauce, lime juice and noodles and mix well.

6 Cook the mixture in the wok for 1 minute, or until heated through and all the ingredients are incorporated.

7 Transfer the noodle and prawn mixture to 4 warmed serving bowls and garnish with slices of lime. Serve immediately.

COOK'S TIP

If available, try using fresh egg noodles. They require very little cooking: simply place in boiling water for 3 minutes, then drain and toss in oil. Noodles can be boiled and eaten plain, or stir-fried with meat and vegetables for a light meal or snack.

Chinese Vegetable Pancakes

Chinese pancakes are made with hardly any fat – they are simply flattened white flour dough.

Nutritional Information
Calories 312
Protein 13g
Carbohydrate 25g
Sugars 5g
Fat 19g
Saturates 7g

INGREDIENTS

1 tbsp vegetable oil

1 garlic clove, crushed

2.5-cm/1-inch piece fresh root ginger, grated

bunch of spring onions, shredded lengthways

100 g/3½ oz mangetout, shredded

225 g/8 oz firm tofu, cut into 1-cm/½-inch pieces (drained weight)

2 tbsp dark soy sauce

2 tbsp hoisin sauce

55 g/2 oz canned bamboo shoots, drained and rinsed

55 g/2 oz canned water chestnuts, drained, rinsed and sliced

100 g/3½ oz beansprouts

1 small fresh red chilli, deseeded and thinly sliced

small bunch of fresh chives

12 soft Chinese pancakes

TO SERVE

shredded Chinese leaves

1 cucumber, sliced

fresh red chilli strips

1 Heat the oil in a preheated wok or a large frying pan. Add the garlic and ginger and stir-fry for 1 minute.

2 Add the spring onions, mangetout, tofu, soy and hoisin sauces. Stir-fry for 2 minutes.

3 Add the bamboo shoots, water chestnuts, beansprouts and chilli to the wok. Stir-fry gently for 2 minutes, until the vegetables are just tender.

4 Snip the fresh chives into 2.5-cm/ 1-inch lengths and stir into the mixture.

5 Heat the Chinese pancakes according to the instructions on the packet and keep warm.

6 Divide the stir-fried vegetables and tofu equally between the Chinese pancakes. Roll up and serve immediately with Chinese leaves, cucumber and chilli strips.

20 MINUTES TO COOK

Peppers & Chestnuts

This is a crunchy and colourful stir-fry, topped with crisp, shredded leeks for both flavour and colour.

Nutritional Informat ɔn
Calories 192
Protein 3g
Carbohydrate 13g
Sugars 5g
Fat 14g
Saturates 13g

INGREDIENTS

225 g/8 oz leeks

vegetable oil, for deep-frying

1 yellow pepper, deseeded and diced

1 green pepper, deseeded and diced

1 red pepper, deseeded and diced

200 g/7 oz canned water chestnuts, drained and sliced

2 garlic cloves, crushed

3 tbsp light soy sauce

1 Thinly shred the leeks. Heat the oil for deep-frying in a preheated wok or large, heavy-based saucepan.

2 Add the leeks to the wok and stir-fry for 2–3 minutes, or until crispy. Remove from the wok with a slotted spoon and drain on kitchen paper. Reserve until required.

3 Pour all but 3 tablespoons of the oil from the wok. Add the yellow, green and red peppers to the wok and stir-fry over a high heat for 5 minutes, or until they begin to brown at the edges and have softened.

4 Add the water chestnuts, garlic and light soy sauce to the wok and stir-fry the vegetables for a further 2–3 minutes.

5 Spoon the pepper stir-fry on to warmed serving plates, sprinkle with the crispy leeks and serve.

COOK'S TIP
Add 1 tablespoon of hoisin sauce with the soy sauce in Step 4 for a richer and spicier flavour.

Semolina Dessert

This dish is eaten with pooris and potato curry for breakfast in northern India. If you like you can serve it with fresh cream for a delicious dessert.

Nutritional Information

Calories 676

Protein 10g

Carbohydrate 96g

Sugars 66g

Fat 31g

Saturates 19g

INGREDIENTS

6 tbsp ghee or vegetable oil

3 cloves

3 cardamoms

8 tbsp coarse semolina

½ tsp saffron threads

50 g/1¾ oz sultanas

2–3 tbsp sugar, or to taste

300 ml/10 fl oz water

300 ml/10 fl oz milk

cream, to serve

TO DECORATE

25 g/1 oz desiccated coconut, toasted

25 g/1 oz chopped almonds

25 g/1 oz pistachio nuts, soaked and chopped (optional)

1 Place the ghee in a saucepan and melt over a medium heat.

2 Add the cloves and cardamoms to the melted butter and reduce the heat, stirring to mix. Add the semolina and stir until it turns a little darker.

3 Add the saffron, sultanas and sugar to the mixture, stirring to mix well.

4 Pour in the water and milk and stir the mixture constantly until the semolina has thickened. Add more water if it becomes too solid.

5 Remove the saucepan from the heat and transfer the semolina to a large serving dish.

6 Decorate the semolina dessert with the toasted desiccated coconut, chopped almonds and pistachio nuts (if using). Serve with a little cream drizzled over the top.

20 MINUTES TO COOK Chocolate Zabaglione

As this recipe only uses a little chocolate, choose one with a minimum of 70 per cent cocoa solids for a really good flavour.

Nutritional Information
Calories 227
Protein 19g
Carbohydrate 29g
Sugars 29g
Fat 9.3g
Saturates 0.4g

INGREDIENTS

4 egg yolks

4 tbsp caster sugar

50 g/1¾ oz plain dark chocolate

125 ml/4 fl oz Marsala wine

amaretti biscuits, to serve

1 Place the egg yolks and caster sugar in a large glass bowl and, using an electric whisk, whisk together until the mixture is very pale.

2 Grate the chocolate finely and fold into the egg mixture.

3 Fold the Marsala wine into the chocolate mixture.

4 Place the glass bowl over a saucepan of gently simmering water and set the electric whisk on the lowest speed or swap to a balloon whisk. Cook gently, whisking constantly, until the mixture thickens. Take care not to overcook or the mixture will curdle.

5 Spoon the hot mixture into warmed individual glass dishes or coffee cups and serve the Zabaglione as soon as possible, while it is warm, light and fluffy, accompanied by amaretti biscuits.

COOK'S TIP
Make the dessert just before serving as it will separate if left to stand. If it begins to curdle, remove it from the heat immediately and place it in a bowl of cold water. Whisk furiously until the mixture comes together.

Warm Fruit Compote

20 MINUTES TO COOK

A bowl of summer fruits suffused with exotic spices releases a burst of flavours on to the palate. The velvety syrup is sure to make this sumptuous dish a firm favourite.

Nutritional Information
Calories 95
Protein 2g
Carbohydrate 21g
Sugars 21g
Fat 0g
Saturates 0g

INGREDIENTS

4 plums, halved and stoned

225 g/8 oz raspberries

225 g/8 oz strawberries, hulled and halved

2 tbsp muscovado sugar

2 tbsp dry white wine

2 star anise

4 cloves

1 cinnamon stick

1 Place all the ingredients in a large, heavy-based saucepan. Cook over a low heat, stirring occasionally, until the sugar has dissolved.

2 Cover tightly and simmer very gently for 5 minutes, or until the fruit is tender but still retains its shape. Do not allow the mixture to boil.

3 Remove and discard the star anise, cloves and cinnamon, and serve the compote warm.

COOK'S TIP
These lightly cooked summer fruits will taste their best if you serve them with a helping of fresh single cream or plain vanilla ice cream.

20 MINUTES TO COOK

Quick Tiramisù

This quick version of one of the most popular Italian desserts is ready in a matter of minutes.

Nutritional Information
Calories 387
Protein 9g
Carbohydrate 22g
Sugars 17g
Fat 28g
Saturates 15g

INGREDIENTS

225 g/8 oz mascarpone or full-fat soft cheese

1 egg, separated

2 tbsp natural yogurt

2 tbsp caster sugar

2 tbsp dark rum

2 tbsp strong black coffee

8 sponge finger biscuits

2 tbsp grated plain dark chocolate

1 Place the cheese in a large bowl, add the egg yolk and yogurt and, using a wooden spoon, beat until smooth.

2 Using a whisk, whisk the egg white in a separate spotlessly clean, greasefree bowl until stiff but not dry, then whisk in the sugar and carefully fold into the cheese mixture.

3 Spoon half of the mixture into 4 tall sundae glasses.

4 Mix the rum and coffee together in a shallow dish. Dip the sponge fingers briefly into the rum mixture, break them in half or into smaller pieces, if necessary, and divide between the glasses.

5 Stir any of the remaining rum and coffee mixture into the remaining cheese and spoon over the top.

6 Sprinkle with grated chocolate and serve immediately. Alternatively, chill in the refrigerator until required.

20 MINUTES TO COOK

Strawberry Baked Alaska

A first choice for children, and even adults will admit to enjoying the contrast between the cold ice cream and the warm meringue in this perennial favourite.

Nutritional Information

Calories 464
Protein 9g
Carbohydrate 63g
Sugars 51g
Fat 21g
Saturates 9g

INGREDIENTS

23-cm/9-inch round sponge cake

2 tbsp sweet sherry or orange juice

5 egg whites

140 g/5 oz caster sugar

600 ml/1 pint strawberry ice cream

175 g/6 oz fresh strawberries, halved, plus
whole strawberries, to serve

1 Preheat the oven to 240°C/475°F/ Gas Mark 9. Place the sponge cake in a large, shallow, ovenproof dish and sprinkle with the sherry or orange juice.

2 Whisk the egg whites in a spotlessly clean, greasefree bowl until stiff. Continue to whisk, gradually adding the sugar, until very stiff and glossy.

3 Working quickly, cover the top of the cake with the ice cream, then top with the strawberry halves. Spread the meringue over the cake, making sure that the ice cream is completely covered. Bake in the preheated oven for 3–5 minutes, or until the meringue is golden brown. Serve immediately, with whole strawberries.

COOK'S TIP
For the perfect meringue, bring the egg whites to room temperature before whisking. It is worth noting that the fresher the eggs, the greater the volume of the meringue.

126

20 MINUTES TO COOK

Quick Syrup Sponge

You won't believe your eyes when you see just how quickly this light-as-air sponge cooks in the microwave oven!

Nutritional Information
Calories 650
Protein 10g
Carbohydrate 89g
Sugars 60g
Fat 31g
Saturates 7g

INGREDIENTS

140 g/5 oz butter or margarine

4 tbsp golden syrup

6 tbsp caster sugar

2 eggs

125 g/4½ oz self-raising flour

1 tsp baking powder

about 2 tbsp warm water

custard, to serve

1 Grease a 1.5-litre/2¾-pint heatproof basin with a small amount of the butter. Spoon the golden syrup into the greased basin.

2 Cream the remaining butter with the sugar until light and fluffy. Gradually add the eggs, beating well after each addition.

3 Sift the flour and baking powder together, then fold into the creamed mixture using a large metal spoon. Add enough water to give a soft, dropping consistency. Spoon into the heatproof basin and smooth the surface.

4 Cover the basin with microwave-proof clingfilm, leaving a small space to let air escape. Microwave on High power for 4 minutes, then remove the sponge from the microwave oven and leave to stand for 5 minutes, while it continues to cook.

5 Turn the sponge out on to a warmed serving plate. Serve with custard.

COOK'S TIP

If you do not have a microwave oven, the sponge can be steamed. Cover the basin with a piece of pleated baking paper and a piece of pleated foil. Place the basin in a saucepan, add boiling water, and steam for 1½ hours.

Apple Fritters

Succulent apple rings, enclosed in crispy batter and sprinkled with cinnamon sugar, are sure to become firm family favourites.

Nutritional Information

Calories 240
Protein 4g
Carbohydrate 37g
Sugars 26g
Fat 10g
Saturates 2g

INGREDIENTS

sunflower oil, for deep-frying
1 large egg
pinch of salt
175 ml/6 fl oz water
55 g/2 oz plain flour
2 tsp ground cinnamon
55 g/2 oz caster sugar
4 eating apples, peeled and cored

1 Pour the sunflower oil into a deep-fryer or large, heavy-based saucepan and heat to 180–190°C/350–375°F, or until a cube of bread browns in 30 seconds.

2 Meanwhile, using an electric mixer, beat the egg and salt together until frothy, then quickly whisk in the water and flour. Do not overbeat the batter – it doesn't matter if it isn't completely smooth.

3 Mix the cinnamon and sugar together in a shallow dish and reserve.

4 Slice the apples into 5-mm/¼-inch thick rings. Spear with a fork, 1 slice at a time, and dip in the batter to coat. Add to the hot oil, in batches, and cook for 1 minute on each side, or until golden and puffed up. Remove with a slotted spoon and drain on kitchen paper. Keep warm while you cook the remaining batches. Transfer to a large serving plate, sprinkle with the cinnamon sugar and serve.

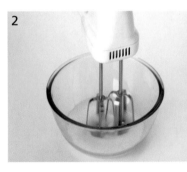

20 MINUTES TO COOK

Grilled Peaches & Cream

Grilled fruit makes a great dessert, not just because it is quick and easy but also because it tastes and looks so delicious.

Nutritional Information
Calories 280
Protein 4g
Carbohydrate 35g
Sugars 35g
Fat 15g
Saturates 9g

INGREDIENTS

4 large peaches

2 tbsp brown sugar

½ tsp ground cinnamon

300 ml/10 fl oz soured cream

4 tbsp caster sugar

1 Preheat the grill to medium. Using a sharp knife, cut the peaches in half and remove the stones, then slice very thinly. Arrange the peach slices in 4 shallow serving dishes.

2 Mix the brown sugar and cinnamon together in a small bowl and sprinkle evenly over the peach slices. Spoon the soured cream over the top, then sprinkle with caster sugar.

3 Place the dishes under the hot grill and cook for 5–6 minutes, or until the sugar is caramelized. Leave to cool for a few minutes, then serve.

COOK'S TIP
To stone peaches, cut vertically around the fruit, then twist each half in opposite directions to reveal the stone. Using the point of a knife, prise the stone out, remove it with your fingers and discard.

20 minutes to cook

If you are after a quick lunch, or you don't want to spend a long time cooking in the evening, then the recipes in this section are perfect. From Capri Salad to Griddled Smoked Salmon you will find it easy to create a delicious meal in 20 minutes.

20

20 MINUTES TO COOK

Aïoli

This garlic mayonnaise features in many traditional Provençal recipes, but also makes a delicious dip, surrounded by a selection of vegetables.

Nutritional Information

Calories 239
Protein 1g
Carbohydrate 1g
Sugars 0g
Fat 26g
Saturates 4g

INGREDIENTS

4 large garlic cloves, or to taste

sea salt and pepper

2 large egg yolks

300 ml/10 fl oz extra virgin olive oil

1–2 tbsp lemon juice

1 tbsp fresh white breadcrumbs

TO SERVE

a selection of raw vegetables, such as sliced red peppers, courgette slices, whole spring onions and tomato wedges

a selection of blanched and cooled vegetables, such as baby artichoke hearts, cauliflower or broccoli florets or French beans

1 Finely chop the garlic on a chopping board. Add a pinch of sea salt to the garlic and use the tip and broad side of the knife to work the garlic and salt into a smooth paste.

2 Transfer the garlic paste to a food processor. Add the egg yolks and process until well blended, scraping down the side of the bowl with a rubber spatula, if necessary.

3 With the motor running, slowly pour the oil in a steady stream through the feeder tube, processing until a thick mayonnaise forms.

4 Add 1 tablespoon of the lemon juice and all the breadcrumbs and process again. Taste and add more lemon juice if necessary. Season to taste with sea salt and pepper.

5 Place the aïoli in a bowl, cover and chill until ready to serve. To serve, place the bowl of aïoli on a large platter and surround with a selection of raw and lightly blanched vegetables.

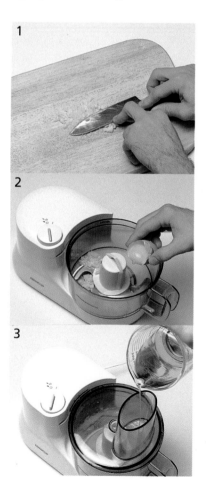

20 MINUTES TO COOK Authentic Guacamole

Guacamole is at its best when freshly made, with enough texture to really taste the avocado. Serve as a sauce for anything Mexican, or dip into it with vegetable sticks or tortilla chips.

Nutritional Information
Calories 212
Protein 2g
Carbohydrate 3g
Sugars 1g
Fat 21g
Saturates 4g

INGREDIENTS

1 ripe tomato

2 limes

2–3 ripe small to medium avocados, or 1–2 large ones

¼–½ onion, finely chopped

pinch of ground cumin

pinch of mild chilli powder

½–1 fresh green chillies, such as jalapeño or serrano, deseeded and finely chopped

1 tbsp finely chopped fresh coriander leaves, plus extra to garnish (optional)

salt (optional)

tortilla chips, to serve (optional)

COOK'S TIP
Avocados grow in abundance in Mexico and guacamole is used to add richness and flavour to all manner of dishes. Try spooning it into soups, especially chicken or seafood, spreading it into sandwiches or stirring it into pan juices for a rich avocado sauce.

1 To peel the tomato, make a small cross to pierce the skin on the base, then place in a heatproof bowl, pour boiling water over to cover and leave to stand for 30 seconds. Drain and plunge into cold water. The skin will then slide off easily. Cut in half, deseed and chop the flesh.

2 Squeeze the juice from the limes into a small non-metallic bowl. Cut one avocado in half around the stone. Twist apart, then remove the stone with a knife. Scoop out the flesh from each half and toss in the bowl of lime juice to prevent discoloration. Repeat with the remaining avocados. Coarsely mash the avocados.

3 Add the tomato, onion, cumin, chilli powder, chillies and coriander to the avocados. If using as a dip for tortilla chips, do not add salt. If using as a sauce, add salt to taste.

4 To serve the guacamole as a dip, transfer to a serving dish, garnish with finely chopped coriander and serve with tortilla chips.

20 MINUTES TO COOK

Spicy Vegetable Soup

Wake up the taste buds with a hint of curry spices in this easy-to-prepare vegetable soup. Served as a light lunch with Indian bread, such as chapati or paratha, it is a healthy option.

Nutritional Information

Calories 75
Protein 3g
Carbohydrate 8g
Sugars 5g
Fat 4g
Saturates 1g

INGREDIENTS

1 tbsp sunflower or corn oil
280 g/10 oz leeks, thinly sliced
2 garlic cloves, finely chopped
½ tsp grated fresh root ginger
½ tsp ground cumin
½ tsp ground coriander
½ tsp ground turmeric
1.2 litres/2 pints vegetable stock
450 g/1 lb tomatoes, finely diced
2 courgettes, cut into batons
salt and pepper
3 tbsp chopped fresh coriander, to garnish

1 Heat the oil in a large, heavy-based saucepan. Add the sliced leeks, chopped garlic and ginger and cook over a medium heat, stirring occasionally, for 2 minutes. Stir in the cumin, ground coriander and turmeric and cook, stirring constantly, for 30 seconds.

2 Pour in the stock and stir well, then bring the mixture to the boil. Reduce the heat, cover and simmer for 5 minutes, then stir in the diced tomatoes and courgette batons. Cover and simmer for a further 3 minutes.

3 Season the soup to taste with salt and pepper, then ladle into 4 warmed serving bowls. Garnish with the chopped fresh coriander and serve.

VARIATION

For a more subtle flavour to this soup, substitute ½ teaspoon crushed saffron threads for the ground turmeric.

Hot & Sour Mushroom Soup

 10 mins

20 mins

serves 4

Hot and sour soups are found across South-east Asia in different forms. Reduce the number of chillies added, if you prefer a milder dish.

Nutritional Information
Calories 87
Protein 4g
Carbohydrate 8g
Sugars 7g
Fat 5g
Saturates 1g

INGREDIENTS

2 tbsp tamarind paste

4 fresh red chillies, very finely chopped

2 garlic cloves, crushed

2 tsp finely chopped fresh root ginger

4 tbsp Thai fish sauce

2 tbsp palm sugar or caster sugar

8 lime leaves, roughly torn

1.25 litres/2 pints vegetable stock

100 g/3½ oz carrots, thinly sliced

225 g/8 oz button mushrooms, halved

350 g/12 oz white cabbage, shredded

100 g/3½ oz fine green beans, halved

3 tbsp roughly chopped fresh coriander

100 g/3½ oz cherry tomatoes, halved

1 Place the tamarind paste, red chillies, garlic, ginger, fish sauce, palm sugar, lime leaves and stock in a large, preheated wok or large, heavy-based saucepan. Bring the mixture to the boil, stirring occasionally.

2 Reduce the heat and add the carrots, mushrooms, white cabbage and green beans. Leave the soup to simmer, uncovered, for 10 minutes, or until the vegetables are tender, but not soft.

3 Stir the fresh coriander and cherry tomatoes into the mixture in the wok and heat through for a further 5 minutes.

4 Transfer the soup to a warmed soup tureen or individual serving bowls and serve immediately.

COOK'S TIP
Tamarind is the dried fruit of the tamarind tree. Sold as a pulp or paste, it is used to give a special sweet and sour flavour to Asian dishes.

Pork & Szechuan Vegetable

30 MINUTES TO COOK

Sold in cans, Szechuan preserved vegetable is pickled mustard root, which is quite hot and salty, so rinse in water before use.

Nutritional Information
Calories 135
Protein 14g
Carbohydrate 3g
Sugars 1g
Fat 7g
Saturates 2g

INGREDIENTS

700 ml/1¼ pints water
250 g/9 oz pork fillet
2 tsp cornflour paste (see page 166)
125 g/4½ oz Szechuan preserved vegetable
salt and pepper
few drops sesame oil (optional)
2–3 spring onions, sliced, to garnish

1 Preheat a wok or large, heavy-based frying pan. Pour in the water and bring to a rolling boil.

2 Using a sharp knife, cut the pork across the grain into thin shreds.

3 Mix the pork with the cornflour paste until the pork is completely coated in the mixture.

4 Thoroughly wash and rinse the Szechuan preserved vegetable, then pat dry on kitchen paper. Cut the Szechuan preserved vegetable into thin shreds the same size as the pork.

5 Add the pork to the wok and stir to separate the shreds. Return to the boil.

6 Add the shredded Szechuan preserved vegetable and return to the boil again.

7 Adjust the seasoning to taste and sprinkle with sesame oil. Serve hot, garnished with spring onions.

30 MINUTES TO COOK Pakoras

Pakoras are eaten all over India. They are made in many different ways and with a variety of fillings. Sometimes they are served in yogurt.

Nutritional Information
Calories 331
Protein 9g
Carbohydrate 27g
Sugars 5g
Fat 22g
Saturates 3g

INGREDIENTS

6 tbsp gram flour

½ tsp salt

1 tsp chilli powder

1 tsp baking powder

1½ tsp white cumin seeds

1 tsp pomegranate seeds

300 ml/10 fl oz water

¼ bunch of fresh coriander, finely chopped

vegetables of your choice: cauliflower, cut into small florets, onions, cut into rings, potatoes, sliced, aubergines, sliced or fresh spinach leaves

vegetable oil, for deep-frying

1 Sift the gram flour into a large bowl. Add the salt, chilli powder, baking powder, cumin and pomegranate seeds and blend together well. Pour in the water and beat well to form a smooth batter.

2 Add the coriander and mix. Leave the batter to stand until required.

3 Dip the prepared vegetables of your choice into the batter, carefully shaking off any excess.

4 Heat the oil for deep-frying in a large, heavy-based frying pan. Place the battered vegetables in the oil and deep-fry, in batches, turning once. Repeat this process until all of the batter has been used up.

5 Transfer the battered vegetables to kitchen paper and drain thoroughly. Serve immediately.

COOK'S TIP
When deep-frying, it is important to use oil at the correct temperature. If the oil is too hot, the outside of the food will burn, as will the spices, before the inside is cooked. If the oil is too cool, the food will be sodden with oil before a crisp batter forms. Draining on kitchen paper is essential as it absorbs excess oil and moisture.

30 MINUTES TO COOK Mussels in White Wine

This soup of mussels, cooked in white wine with onions and cream, can be served as an appetizer or a main dish with plenty of crusty bread.

Nutritional Information
Calories 396
Protein 23g
Carbohydrate 8g
Sugars 2g
Fat 24g
Saturates 15g

INGREDIENTS

about 3 litres/5¼ pints fresh mussels

55 g/2 oz butter

1 large onion, very finely chopped

2–3 garlic cloves, crushed

350 ml/12 fl oz dry white wine

150 ml/5 fl oz water

2 tbsp lemon juice

good pinch of finely grated lemon rind

1 bouquet garni

salt and pepper

1 tbsp plain flour

4 tbsp single or double cream

2–3 tbsp chopped fresh parsley

crusty bread, to serve

1 Pull off all the 'beards' from the mussels and scrub them thoroughly under cold running water for 5 minutes to remove all mud, sand and barnacles, etc. Discard any mussels that refuse to close when sharply tapped with a knife.

2 Melt half the butter in a large saucepan over a low heat. Add the onion and garlic and fry gently until softened, but not coloured.

3 Add the wine, water, lemon juice and rind and bouquet garni. Season to taste with salt and pepper. Bring to the boil over a low heat, then cover and simmer for 4–5 minutes.

4 Add the mussels to the saucepan, cover tightly and simmer for 5 minutes, shaking the saucepan frequently, until all the mussels have opened. Discard any mussels that have not opened. Remove the bouquet garni and discard.

5 Remove mussels from the pan and keep warm. Blend the remaining butter with the flour and whisk into the liquid, a little at a time. Simmer gently for 2–3 minutes, or until slightly thickened.

6 Add the cream and half the parsley to the soup and reheat gently. Adjust the seasoning, if necessary. Ladle the mussels and liquid into 4 large, warmed soup bowls, sprinkle with the remaining parsley and serve with crusty bread.

30 MINUTES TO COOK

Smoked Fish & Potato Pâté

This delicious smoked fish pâté is given a tart fruity flavour by the cooked gooseberries, which complement the fish perfectly.

Nutritional Information

Calories 418

Protein 18g

Carbohydrate 32g

Sugars 4g

Fat 25g

Saturates 6g

INGREDIENTS

650 g/1 lb 7 oz floury potatoes, peeled and diced

300 g/10½ oz smoked mackerel, skinned and flaked

75 g/2¾ oz cooked gooseberries

2 tsp lemon juice

2 tbsp low-fat crème fraîche

1 tbsp capers, drained

1 gherkin, chopped

1 tbsp chopped pickled dill cucumber

1 tbsp chopped fresh dill

salt and pepper

lemon wedges, to garnish

warm crusty bread, to serve

1 Bring a saucepan of water to the boil over a medium heat. Add the potatoes and cook for 10 minutes, or until tender. Drain thoroughly.

2 Place the cooked potatoes in a food processor or blender. Add the smoked mackerel and process for 30 seconds, or until fairly smooth. Alternatively, place the ingredients in a large bowl and mash with a fork.

3 Add the gooseberries, lemon juice and crème fraîche to the fish and potato mixture. Blend for a further 10 seconds or mash well.

4 Stir in the capers, gherkin, dill cucumber and fresh dill. Season to taste with salt and pepper.

5 Transfer the fish pâté to a serving dish and garnish with lemon wedges. Serve with slices of warm crusty bread.

2

3

4

Sweet Potato Salad

30 MINUTES TO COOK

This unusual salad, with its peppery dressing, is best eaten while it is still warm. It is full of protein and vitamins, and can be served on its own or with crusty bread as a satisfying light meal.

Nutritional Information
Calories 192
Protein 7g
Carbohydrate 33g
Sugars 23g
Fat 4g
Saturates 1g

INGREDIENTS

1 sweet potato, peeled and diced

2 carrots, sliced

3 tomatoes, deseeded and chopped

85 g/3 oz canned chickpeas, drained

8 iceberg lettuce leaves

1 tbsp sultanas

1 tbsp chopped walnuts

1 small onion, thinly sliced into rings

DRESSING

6 tbsp natural yogurt

1 tbsp clear honey

1 tsp coarsely ground pepper

salt

1 Cook the sweet potato in a large saucepan of boiling water for 10 minutes. Add the carrots and cook for a further 3–5 minutes, or until the sweet potato is tender, but still firm to the bite. Drain well and place in a large bowl. Add the chopped tomatoes and chickpeas to the sweet potato and carrots and mix together thoroughly.

2 Line a salad bowl with the lettuce leaves and spoon the vegetable mixture into the centre. Sprinkle with the sultanas, walnuts and onion rings.

3 To make the dressing, place the yogurt, honey and pepper in a small serving bowl and whisk thoroughly with a fork. Season with salt to taste. Serve the sweet potato salad warm and hand around the dressing separately.

30 MINUTES TO COOK   Lobster Salad

Lobsters are best prepared extremely simply to ensure that none of the rich, sweet flavour is lost amid a mass of other ingredients.

Nutritional Information

Calories 487
Protein 24g
Carbohydrate 2g
Sugars 2g
Fat 42g
Saturates 6g

INGREDIENTS

2 raw lobster tails

LEMON-DILL MAYONNAISE

1 large lemon

1 large egg yolk

½ tsp Dijon mustard

150 ml/5 fl oz olive oil

salt and pepper

1 tbsp chopped fresh dill

TO GARNISH

radicchio leaves

lemon wedges

fresh dill sprigs

1 To make the mayonnaise, finely grate the lemon rind and squeeze the juice. Beat the egg yolk in a small bowl and beat in the mustard and 1 teaspoon of the lemon juice.

2 Using a balloon whisk or electric mixer, beat in the olive oil, drop by drop, until a thick mayonnaise forms. Stir in half the lemon rind and 1 tablespoon of the juice.

3 Season with salt and pepper and add more lemon juice if desired. Stir in the dill and cover with clingfilm. Chill in the refrigerator until required.

4 Bring a large saucepan of lightly salted water to the boil. Add the lobster tails, return to the boil and cook for 6 minutes, until the flesh is opaque and the shells are red. Drain immediately and leave to cool.

5 Remove the lobster flesh from the shells and cut into bite-sized pieces. Arrange the radicchio leaves on individual serving plates and top with the lobster flesh. Place a spoonful of the mayonnaise on the side. Garnish with lemon wedges and fresh dill sprigs and serve.

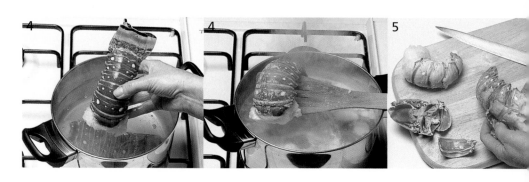

Chargrilled Chicken Salad

30 MINUTES TO COOK

This is a quick starter to serve at a barbecue – if the bread is bent in half, the chicken salad can be put in the centre and eaten as finger food.

Nutritional Information
Calories 225
Protein 16g
Carbohydrate 15g
Sugars 5g
Fat 12g
Saturates 2g

INGREDIENTS

2 skinless, boneless chicken breasts

1 red onion

sunflower oil, for brushing

1 avocado, peeled and stoned

1 tbsp lemon juice

125 ml/4 fl oz low-fat mayonnaise

¼ tsp chilli powder

¼ tsp salt

½ tsp pepper

4 tomatoes, quartered

½ loaf sun-dried tomato focaccia bread

green salad, to serve

1 Preheat the barbecue. Cut the chicken breasts into 1-cm/½-inch strips.

2 Cut the onion into 8 pieces, held together at the root. Rinse under cold running water, then brush with oil.

3 Purée or mash the avocado and lemon juice together. Whisk in the mayonnaise. Add the chilli powder and season with the salt and pepper.

4 Place the chicken and onion over hot coals and barbecue for 3–4 minutes on each side. Combine the chicken, onion, tomatoes and avocado mixture.

5 Cut the bread in half horizontally and then into 4 pieces. Toast on the hot barbecue for 2 minutes on each side.

6 Spoon the chicken mixture on to the focaccia toasts and serve immediately with a green salad.

VARIATION
Instead of focaccia, serve the salad in pitta breads, which have been warmed through on the side of the barbecue.

Spaghetti alla Carbonara

30 MINUTES TO COOK

Ensure that all of the cooked ingredients are as hot as possible before adding the eggs, so that they cook on contact.

Nutritional Information
Calories 1092
Protein 37g
Carbohydrate 86g
Sugars 9g
Fat 69g
Saturates 36g

INGREDIENTS

425 g/15 oz dried spaghetti

salt and pepper

fresh sage sprigs, to garnish

freshly grated Parmesan cheese, to serve (optional)

SAUCE

1 tbsp olive oil

1 large onion, thinly sliced

2 garlic cloves, chopped

175 g/6 oz rindless bacon, cut into thin strips

2 tbsp butter

175 g/6 oz mushrooms, sliced

300 ml/10 fl oz double cream

3 eggs, beaten

100 g/3½ oz freshly grated Parmesan cheese

1 Warm a large serving dish or bowl. To cook the pasta, bring a large saucepan of lightly salted water to the boil. Add the spaghetti, return to the boil and cook for 8–10 minutes, until tender but still firm to the bite. Drain well and keep warm.

2 Meanwhile, to make the sauce, heat the olive oil in a frying pan. Add the onion and cook, stirring occasionally, for 2–3 minutes, until translucent. Add the garlic and bacon and cook until the bacon is crisp. Transfer to the warmed dish or bowl.

3 Melt the butter in the frying pan. Add the mushrooms and cook over a medium heat, stirring occasionally, for 3–4 minutes, until tender. Return the bacon mixture to the frying pan. Cover and keep warm.

4 Combine the cream, eggs and cheese in a large bowl and season to taste.

5 Working very quickly, tip the spaghetti into the bacon mixture and pour over the egg mixture. Toss the spaghetti quickly into the mixture, using 2 forks, and serve immediately, garnished with sage. If you wish, serve with extra Parmesan cheese.

COOK'S TIP
The key to success with this recipe is not to overcook the egg. That is why it is important to keep all the ingredients hot enough to just cook the egg and to work rapidly to avoid scrambling it.

30 MINUTES TO COOK   Speedy Peanut Pan-fry

A complete main course cooked within thirty minutes. Thread egg noodles are the ideal accompaniment because they can be cooked quickly and easily while the stir-fry sizzles.

Nutritional Information
Calories 563
Protein 45g
Carbohydrate 22g
Sugars 7g
Fat 33g
Saturates 7g

INGREDIENTS

300 g/10½ oz courgettes

250 g/9 oz baby corn cobs

300 g/10½ oz button mushrooms

salt and pepper

250 g/9 oz thread egg noodles

2 tbsp sunflower oil

1 tbsp sesame oil

8 boneless chicken thighs or 4 breasts, thinly sliced

350 g/12 oz beansprouts

4 tbsp smooth peanut butter

2 tbsp soy sauce

2 tbsp lime or lemon juice

55 g/2 oz roasted peanuts

fresh coriander sprigs, to garnish

1 Using a sharp knife, thinly slice the courgettes, baby corn cobs and mushrooms.

2 Bring a large saucepan of lightly salted boiling water to the boil. Add the noodles and cook for 3–4 minutes. Meanwhile, heat the sunflower oil and sesame oil in a large frying pan or preheated wok. Add the chicken and fry over a fairly high heat for 1 minute.

3 Add the sliced courgettes, baby corn cobs and mushrooms and stir-fry for 5 minutes. Add the beansprouts, peanut butter, soy sauce, lime juice and pepper to taste, then cook for a further 2 minutes.

4 Drain the noodles, transfer to a serving dish and sprinkle with the peanuts. Serve with the stir-fried chicken and vegetables, garnished with fresh coriander sprigs.

Stir-fried Ginger Chicken

30 MINUTES TO COOK

The orange adds colour and piquancy to this refreshing dish, and is an ideal partner to chicken.

Nutritional Information
Calories 289
Protein 20g
Carbohydrate 17g
Sugars 15g
Fat 9g
Saturates 2g

INGREDIENTS

2 tbsp sunflower oil

1 onion, sliced

175 g/6 oz carrots, cut into matchsticks

1 garlic clove, crushed

350 g/12 oz skinless, boneless chicken breasts

2 tbsp grated fresh root ginger

1 tsp ground ginger

4 tbsp sweet sherry

1 tbsp tomato purée

1 tbsp demerara sugar

100 ml/3½ fl oz orange juice

1 tsp cornflour

1 orange, peeled and segmented

fresh snipped chives, to garnish

1 Heat the oil in a preheated wok or large, heavy-based frying pan. Add the onion, carrots and garlic and stir-fry over a high heat for 3 minutes, or until the vegetables begin to soften.

2 Cut the chicken into thin strips, then add to the wok with the fresh and ground ginger. Stir-fry for a further 10 minutes, or until the chicken is well cooked through and golden in colour.

3 Mix the sherry, tomato purée, sugar, orange juice and cornflour together in a bowl. Stir the mixture into the wok and heat through until the mixture bubbles and the juices begin to thicken.

4 Add the orange segments and carefully toss to mix.

5 Transfer the stir-fried chicken to warmed serving bowls and garnish with fresh snipped chives. Serve immediately.

Thai-style Burgers

30 MINUTES TO COOK

If your family likes to eat burgers, try these – they have a much more interesting flavour than the conventional hamburgers!

Nutritional Information
Calories 358
Protein 23g
Carbohydrate 2g
Sugars 1g
Fat 29g
Saturates 5g

INGREDIENTS

1 small lemon grass stalk
1 small fresh red chilli, deseeded
2 garlic cloves
2 spring onions
200 g/7 oz closed-cup mushrooms
400 g/14 oz lean pork mince
1 tbsp Thai fish sauce
3 tbsp chopped fresh coriander
salt and pepper
plain flour, for dusting
sunflower oil, for shallow-frying
2 tbsp mayonnaise
1 tbsp lime juice
TO SERVE
4 sesame hamburger buns
shredded Chinese leaves

1 Place the lemon grass, chilli, garlic and spring onions in a food processor and process to form a smooth paste. Add the mushrooms and process until very finely chopped.

2 Add the pork, fish sauce and coriander. Season well with salt and pepper, then divide the mixture into 4 equal portions and form with lightly floured hands into flat burger shapes.

3 Heat the oil in a frying pan over a medium heat. Add the burgers and fry for 6–8 minutes, until cooked through.

4 Meanwhile, mix the mayonnaise with the lime juice in a small bowl. Split the hamburger buns and spread the lime-flavoured mayonnaise on the cut surfaces. Add a few shredded Chinese leaves, top with a cooked burger and sandwich together. Serve immediately while still hot.

30 MINUTES TO COOK

Yellow Curry

Potatoes are not highly regarded in Thai cooking because rice is the traditional staple food, but this dish is a tasty exception.

Nutritional Information
Calories 160
Protein 3g
Carbohydrate 15g
Sugars 4g
Fat 10g
Saturates 1g

INGREDIENTS

2 garlic cloves, finely chopped

3-cm/1¼-inch piece fresh root ginger or galangal, finely chopped

1 lemon grass stalk, finely chopped

1 tsp coriander seeds

3 tbsp vegetable oil

2 tsp Thai red curry paste

½ tsp ground turmeric

200 ml/7 fl oz coconut milk

250 g/9 oz potatoes, cut into cubes

100 ml/3½ fl oz vegetable stock

200 g/7 oz fresh young spinach leaves

1 small onion, thinly sliced into rings

1 Place the garlic, ginger, lemon grass and coriander seeds in a mortar and crush with a pestle to a smooth paste.

2 Heat 2 tablespoons of the oil in a preheated wok or large, heavy-based frying pan. Add the fresh garlic and spice paste and stir-fry over a high heat for 30 seconds, then stir in the curry paste and turmeric, add the coconut milk and bring to the boil.

3 Add the potatoes and stock. Return to the boil, then reduce the heat and simmer, uncovered, for 10–12 minutes, or until the potatoes are almost tender.

4 Stir in the spinach and simmer until the leaves have wilted.

5 Heat the remaining oil in a separate frying pan. Add the onion and cook until crisp and golden brown. Place on top of the curry just before serving.

30 MINUTES TO COOK

Tofu Casserole

Although mild in flavour, tofu will absorb the other flavours in this dish. If marinated tofu is used, it will also add a flavour of its own.

Nutritional Information
Calories 228
Protein 16g
Carbohydrate 7g
Sugars 3g
Fat 15g
Saturates 2g

INGREDIENTS

2 tbsp groundnut oil

8 spring onions, cut into batons

2 celery sticks, sliced

125 g/4½ oz broccoli florets

125 g/4½ oz courgettes, sliced

2 garlic cloves, thinly sliced

450 g/1 lb fresh baby spinach leaves

450 g/1 lb tofu, cut into 2.5-cm/1-inch cubes (drained weight)

SAUCE

425 ml/15 fl oz vegetable stock

2 tbsp light soy sauce

3 tbsp hoisin sauce

½ tsp chilli powder

1 tbsp sesame oil

1 Heat the groundnut oil in a preheated wok or large, heavy-based frying pan.

2 Add the spring onions, celery, broccoli, courgettes, garlic, spinach and tofu to the wok and stir-fry for 3–4 minutes.

3 To make the sauce, mix the stock, soy sauce, hoisin sauce, chilli powder and sesame oil together in a small flameproof casserole and bring to the boil.

4 Add the stir-fried vegetables and tofu to the casserole, reduce the heat, then cover and simmer for 10 minutes.

5 Transfer the tofu and vegetables to a warmed serving dish and serve.

COOK'S TIP
This recipe incorporates mainly green vegetables, but you could alter them according to likes and dislikes. Add mushrooms, carrots, baby corn cobs or Chinese leaves, if preferred.

Lamb Meatballs

These small meatballs are made with minced lamb and flavoured with chilli, garlic, parsley and Chinese curry powder.

Nutritional Information

Calories 320
Protein 28g
Carbohydrate 8g
Sugars 1g
Fat 20g
Saturates 6g

INGREDIENTS

450 g/1 lb fresh lamb mince
3 garlic cloves, crushed
2 spring onions, finely chopped
½ tsp chilli powder
1 tsp Chinese curry powder
1 tbsp chopped fresh parsley
25 g/1 oz fresh white breadcrumbs
1 egg, beaten
3 tbsp vegetable oil
125 g/4½ oz Chinese leaves, shredded
1 leek, sliced
1 tbsp cornflour
2 tbsp water
300 ml/10 fl oz lamb stock
1 tbsp dark soy sauce
shredded leek, to garnish

1 Mix the lamb, garlic, spring onions, chilli powder, Chinese curry powder, parsley and breadcrumbs together in a bowl. Stir in the egg and mix to form a firm mixture. Using your hands roll into 16 small, even-sized balls.

2 Heat the oil in a preheated wok or large, heavy-based frying pan. Add the Chinese leaves and leek and stir-fry for 1 minute. Remove from the wok with a slotted spoon and reserve. Add the meatballs to the wok and fry in batches, turning gently, for 3–4 minutes, or until golden brown.

3 Mix the cornflour and water together to form a smooth paste and reserve. Pour the stock and soy sauce into the wok and cook for 2–3 minutes. Stir in the cornflour paste. Bring to the boil and cook, stirring constantly, until the sauce has thickened.

4 Return the Chinese leaves and leek to the wok and cook for 1 minute, until heated through. Arrange the Chinese leaves and leek in a warmed serving dish, then top with the meatballs, garnish with the shredded leek and serve.

Pork Chops with Sage

 10 mins

15 mins

serves 4

The fresh taste of sage is the perfect ingredient to counteract the richness of the pork in this quick and simple dish.

Nutritional Information

Calories 364
Protein 34g
Carbohydrate 14g
Sugars 5g
Fat 19g
Saturates 7g

INGREDIENTS

2 tbsp flour

1 tbsp chopped fresh sage or 1 tsp dried sage

salt and pepper

4 boneless, lean pork chops, trimmed of excess fat

2 tbsp olive oil

15 g/½ oz butter

2 red onions, sliced into rings

1 tbsp lemon juice

2 tsp caster sugar

4 plum tomatoes, quartered

green salad, to serve

1 Mix the flour, sage and salt and pepper to taste on a large plate. Lightly dust the pork chops on both sides with the seasoned flour.

2 Heat the oil and butter in a large frying pan. Add the pork chops and cook for 6–7 minutes on each side until cooked through. Drain the pork chops, reserving the pan juices and keep warm.

3 Toss the onion in the lemon juice and add to the frying pan. Fry with the sugar and tomatoes for 5 minutes, until tender.

4 Transfer the pork chops to 4 warmed serving plates and pour over the pan juices. Serve with the tomato and onion mixture and a green salad.

30 MINUTES TO COOK   Chilli Coconut Chicken

This delicious Thai-style dish has a classic sauce of lime, peanut, coconut and red chilli.

Nutritional Information
Calories 348
Protein 36g
Carbohydrate 3g
Sugars 2g
Fat 21g
Saturates 8g

INGREDIENTS

150 ml/5 fl oz hot Chicken Stock

25 g/1 oz creamed coconut

1 tbsp sunflower oil

8 skinless, boneless chicken thighs, cut into long, thin strips

1 small fresh red chilli, thinly sliced

4 spring onions, thinly sliced

4 tbsp smooth or crunchy peanut butter

finely grated rind and juice of 1 lime

freshly cooked rice, to serve

TO GARNISH

spring onion tassels

fresh red chillies

1 Place the stock in a measuring jug and crumble the creamed coconut into the stock, stirring to dissolve.

2 Heat the oil in a large, heavy-based frying pan or a preheated wok. Add the chicken strips and cook, stirring, until golden.

3 Add the sliced red chilli and the spring onions to the frying pan and cook gently for a few minutes, stirring to mix all the ingredients.

VARIATION
Serve jasmine rice with this spicy dish. It has a fragrant aroma that is well suited to Thai-style recipes.

4 Add the peanut butter, coconut mixture, lime rind and juice and simmer uncovered, stirring, for 5 minutes. Serve with rice, garnished with a spring onion tassel and a red chilli.

170

30 MINUTES TO COOK Pork with Mooli

Mooli is a long, white root vegetable with a similar flavour to radish. It can be found in most large supermarkets.

Nutritional Information
Calories 280
Protein 25g
Carbohydrate 2g
Sugars 1g
Fat 19g
Saturates 4g

INGREDIENTS

4 tbsp vegetable oil

450 g/1 lb pork tenderloin

1 aubergine, diced

2 garlic cloves, crushed

225 g/8 oz mooli

3 tbsp soy sauce

2 tbsp sweet chilli sauce

freshly cooked rice or noodles, to serve

1 Heat 2 tablespoons of the oil in a preheated wok or large, heavy-based frying pan.

2 Cut the pork into bite-sized pieces, then add to the wok and stir-fry for 5 minutes.

3 Add the remaining vegetable oil to the wok. Add the aubergine together with the garlic and stir-fry for 5 minutes.

4 Slice the mooli and add to the wok. Stir-fry for 2 minutes.

5 Stir the soy sauce and sweet chilli sauce into the mixture in the wok and cook until heated through.

6 Transfer the pork and mooli to warmed serving bowls and serve immediately with rice or noodles.

10 mins

 15 mins

 serves 4

30 MINUTES TO COOK Stir-fried Cod with Mango

Fish and fruit are a classic combination, and this dish is no exception with its tropical fruity flavour.

Nutritional Information
Calories 200
Protein 21g
Carbohydrate 14g
Sugars 12g
Fat 7g
Saturates 1g

INGREDIENTS

175 g/6 oz carrots
2 tbsp vegetable oil
1 red onion, sliced
1 red pepper, deseeded and sliced
1 green pepper, deseeded and sliced
1 ripe mango
450 g/1 lb skinless cod fillet, cubed
1 tsp cornflour
1 tbsp light soy sauce
100 ml/3½ fl oz tropical fruit juice
1 tbsp lime juice
1 tbsp chopped fresh coriander, to garnish

1 Thinly slice the carrots. Heat the oil in a preheated wok or large, heavy-based frying pan. Add the onion, carrots and peppers and stir-fry for 5 minutes.

2 Peel, stone and slice the mango, then add to the wok with the cod. Stir-fry for a further 4–5 minutes, or until the fish is cooked through. (Be careful not to break up the fish.)

3 Mix the cornflour, soy sauce, fruit juice and lime juice together. Pour the mixture into the wok and stir until the mixture bubbles and the juices thicken. Sprinkle with coriander and serve.

COOK'S TIP
You can use pawpaw as an alternative to the mango, if you prefer.

174

30 MINUTES TO COOK Indonesian-style Spicy Cod

A delicious aromatic coating makes this dish rather special. Serve it with a crisp salad and crusty bread.

Nutritional Information
Calories 146
Protein 19g
Carbohydrate 2g
Sugars 2g
Fat 7g
Saturates 4g

INGREDIENTS

1 lemon grass stalk, outer leaves removed
1 small red onion, chopped
3 garlic cloves, chopped
2 fresh red chillies, deseeded and chopped
1 tsp grated fresh root ginger
¼ tsp ground turmeric
salt and pepper
2 tbsp butter, cut into small cubes
8 tbsp canned coconut milk
2 tbsp lemon juice
4 cod steaks
fresh red chillies, to garnish (optional)
mixed leaf salad, to serve

1 Preheat the barbecue. Thinly slice the lemon grass, then place in a food processor with the onion, garlic, chillies, ginger and turmeric. Process until finely chopped. Season to taste with salt and pepper.

2 With the processor still running, add the butter, coconut milk and lemon juice and process until well blended.

3 Place the fish in a shallow, non-metallic dish. Pour the coconut mixture over the fish and turn until well coated.

4 Place the cod in a hinged rack, if you have one, which will make them easier to turn. Barbecue over hot coals for 15 minutes, or until the fish is cooked through, turning once. Serve garnished with red chillies (if using) and salad leaves.

COOK'S TIP
If you prefer a milder flavour, omit the chillies altogether. For a hotter flavour do not remove the seeds from the chillies.

176

Asparagus & Red Pepper Parcels

30 MINUTES TO COOK

These small parcels are ideal as part of a main meal and irresistible as a quick snack with extra plum sauce for dipping.

Nutritional Information
Calories 194
Protein 3g
Carbohydrate 11g
Sugars 2g
Fat 16g
Saturates 4g

INGREDIENTS

1 red pepper, deseeded
100 g/3½ oz fine tip asparagus
50 g/1¾ oz beansprouts
2 tbsp plum sauce
1 egg yolk
8 sheets filo pastry
vegetable oil, for deep-frying
sweet chilli dipping sauce, to serve

1 Slice the red pepper and cut the asparagus into pieces. Place with the beansprouts in a large bowl.

2 Add the plum sauce to the vegetables and mix thoroughly.

3 Beat the egg yolk lightly in a small bowl and reserve until required.

4 Spread out the sheets of filo pastry on a work surface and work on them one at a time.

5 Place a little of the asparagus and red pepper filling one end of each filo pastry sheet. Brush the edges of the filo pastry with a little of the beaten egg yolk.

6 Roll up the filo pastry, tucking in the ends and enclosing the filling like a spring roll. Repeat with the remaining filo sheets.

7 Heat the oil for deep-frying in a large preheated wok. Carefully cook the parcels, 2 at a time, in the hot oil for 4–5 minutes, or until crisp.

8 Remove the deep-fried parcels with a slotted spoon and drain on kitchen paper.

9 Transfer the parcels to warmed serving plates and serve immediately with the dipping sauce.

COOK'S TIP
Be sure to use fine-tipped asparagus, as it is more tender than the larger stems.

30 MINUTES TO COOK **Barbecue Mushrooms**

*Large mushrooms have more flavour
than the smaller button mushrooms.
Serve these mushrooms as part of a
vegetarian barbecue.*

Nutritional Information
Calories 148
Protein 11g
Carbohydrate 11g
Sugars 1g
Fat 7g
Saturates 3g

INGREDIENTS

12 open-cap mushrooms

4 tsp olive oil

4 spring onions, chopped

100 g/3½ oz fresh brown breadcrumbs

1 tsp chopped fresh oregano

100 g/3½ oz low-fat mature Cheddar cheese

1 Preheat the barbecue or the oven to
180°C/350°F/Gas Mark 4. Remove the
stalks from the mushrooms, reserving
the caps. Chop the stalks finely.

2 Heat half the oil in a frying pan. Add
the mushroom stalks and spring onions
and cook over a low heat, stirring
occasionally, for 5 minutes.

3 Transfer the mushroom stalks and
spring onions to a large bowl with a
slotted spoon and add the
breadcrumbs and oregano. Mix well.

4 Crumble the cheese into small
pieces, then add to the breadcrumb
mixture and mix well. Spoon the
mixture into the mushroom caps.

VARIATION
**For a change, replace the cheese with
chopped hard-boiled eggs or chopped
olives. Mop up the juices with some
crusty bread.**

5 Drizzle the remaining oil over the
stuffed mushrooms. Barbecue the
mushrooms on an oiled rack over
medium–hot coals for 10 minutes,
or until cooked through. Alternatively,
arrange on a baking sheet and bake
in the preheated oven for 20 minutes,
or until cooked through.

6 Transfer the mushrooms to serving
plates and serve hot.

30 MINUTES TO COOK

Exotic Fruit Salad

This is a sophisticated fruit salad that makes use of some of the exotic fruits that can now be seen in supermarkets.

Nutritional Information
Calories 149
Protein 1g
Carbohydrate 39g
Sugars 39g
Fat 0.1g
Saturates 0g

INGREDIENTS

3 passion fruit

125 g/4 oz caster sugar

150 ml/5 fl oz water

1 mango

10 lychees, canned or fresh

1 star fruit

1 Halve the passion fruit and press the flesh through a sieve into a saucepan.

2 Add the sugar and water and bring to a gentle boil, stirring.

3 Place the mango on a chopping board and cut a slice from either side, cutting as near to the stone as possible. Cut away as much flesh as possible in large chunks from the stone section.

4 Take the 2 side slices and make 3 cuts through the flesh but not the skin, and 3 more at right angles to make a lattice pattern.

5 Push the mango skin inside out so that the cubed flesh is exposed and you can easily cut it off.

6 Peel and stone the lychees and cut the star fruit into 12 slices.

7 Add all the mango flesh, the lychees and the star fruit to the passion fruit syrup and poach gently for 5 minutes. Remove the fruit with a slotted spoon.

8 Bring the syrup to the boil and cook for 5 minutes, until it thickens slightly.

9 To serve, transfer all the fruit to individual serving glasses, pour over the sugar syrup and serve warm.

COOK'S TIP
A delicious accompaniment to any exotic fruit dish is cardamom cream. Crush the seeds from 2 cardamom pods, add 300 ml/10 fl oz whipping cream and whip until soft peaks form.

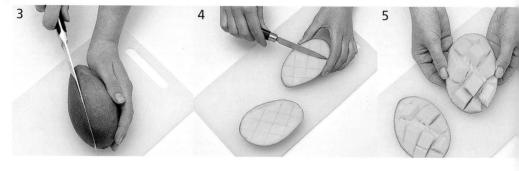

182

30 MINUTES TO COOK Sweet Fruit Wontons

These sweet wontons are very adaptable and may be filled with whole, small fruits or a spicy chopped mixture, as here.

Nutritional Information
Calories 244
Protein 2g
Carbohydrate 35g
Sugars 25g
Fat 12g
Saturates 3g

INGREDIENTS

12 wonton wrappers
2 tsp cornflour
6 tsp cold water
vegetable oil, for deep-frying
2 tbsp clear honey
selection of fresh fruit (such as kiwi fruit, limes, oranges, mango and apples), sliced, to serve

FILLING
175 g/6 oz dried stoned dates, chopped
2 tsp dark brown sugar
½ tsp ground cinnamon

1 To make the filling, mix the dates, sugar and cinnamon together.

2 Spread out the wonton wrappers on a chopping board and spoon a little of the filling into the centre of each wrapper.

3 Blend the cornflour and water together and brush this mixture around the edges of the wrappers.

4 Fold the wrappers over the filling, bringing the edges together, then bring the 2 corners together, sealing with the cornflour mixture.

5 Heat the oil for deep-frying in a wok to 180°C/350°F, or until a cube of bread browns in 30 seconds. Fry the wontons, in batches, for 2–3 minutes, until golden. Remove the wontons from the oil with a slotted spoon and leave to drain on kitchen paper.

6 Place the honey in a bowl and stand it in warm water, to soften it slightly. Drizzle the honey over the sweet fruit wontons and serve with a selection of fresh fruit.

Cherry Pancakes

30 MINUTES TO COOK

This dish is made with canned cherries for extra speed, but you could use fresh stoned cherries if you have more time.

Nutritional Information
Calories 345
Protein 8g
Carbohydrate 56g
Sugars 25g
Fat 11g
Saturates 2g

INGREDIENTS

FILLING
400 g/14 oz canned stoned cherries, plus juice
½ tsp almond essence
½ tsp ground mixed spice
2 tbsp cornflour
PANCAKES
100 g/3½ oz plain flour
pinch of salt
2 tbsp chopped fresh mint
1 egg
300 ml/10 fl oz milk
vegetable oil, for frying
TO DECORATE
icing sugar
toasted flaked almonds

1 Place the cherries and 300 ml/ 10 fl oz of the juice in a saucepan with the almond essence and mixed spice. Stir in the cornflour and bring to the boil, stirring, until thickened and clear. Reserve until required.

2 To make the pancakes, sift the flour into a bowl with the salt. Add the chopped mint and make a well in the centre. Gradually beat in the egg and milk to form a smooth batter.

3 Heat 1 tablespoon oil in an 18-cm/ 7-inch frying pan. Pour off the oil when hot. Add just enough batter to coat the base of the frying pan and cook for 1–2 minutes, or until the underside is cooked. Flip the pancake over and cook for 1 minute. Remove the pancake from the frying pan and keep warm. Heat another 1 tablespoon of the oil in the frying pan and repeat to use up all the batter.

4 Spoon a quarter of the cherry filling on to one quarter of each pancake and fold the pancake into a cone shape. Dust with icing sugar and sprinkle the flaked almonds over the top. Serve.

VARIATION
Use other fillings, such as blackberries or gooseberries, as an alternative to the cherries.

Pancake Pieces

This is a cheap and cheerful, easy-to-make dessert that is perfect for midweek family suppers. Its casual presentation makes it a favourite with children.

Nutritional Information

Calories 306
Protein 8g
Carbohydrate 50g
Sugars 26g
Fat 10g
Saturates 2g

INGREDIENTS

2 tbsp caster sugar

1 tsp ground cinnamon

125 g/4½ oz plain flour

pinch of salt

2 eggs, lightly beaten

125 ml/4 fl oz milk

400 g/14 oz canned apricot halves in syrup

sunflower oil, for brushing

1 Place the sugar and cinnamon in a bowl, stir to mix and reserve.

2 Sift the flour and salt into a separate bowl. Whisk the eggs and milk into the flour and continue whisking to make a smooth batter.

3 Drain the apricot halves, reserving the syrup, then whisk the syrup into the batter until combined. Roughly chop the apricots and reserve.

4 Heat a large crêpe pan or heavy-based frying pan and brush with oil. Pour in the batter and cook over a medium heat for 4–5 minutes, or until the underside is golden brown. Turn over with a palette knife and cook the second side for 4 minutes, or until golden. Tear the pancake into bite-sized pieces with 2 spoons or forks.

5 Add the apricots to the crêpe pan and heat through briefly. Divide the pancake pieces and apricots between 4 serving plates, sprinkle with the sugar and cinnamon mixture and serve immediately.

COOK'S TIP
Before you add the batter to the frying pan, make sure the oil is very hot. Tilt and roll the frying pan as you pour the batter in, to spread it over the base in a thin layer.

Ginger & Apricot Alaskas

No ice cream in this Alaska but a mixture of apples and apricots poached in orange juice and enclosed in meringue.

Nutritional Information

Calories 442

Protein 7g

Carbohydrate 83g

Sugars 77g

Fat 9g

Saturates 3g

INGREDIENTS

2 slices rich, dark ginger cake, about 2 cm/¾ inch thick

1–2 tbsp ginger wine or rum

1 apple

6 ready-to-eat dried apricots, chopped

4 tbsp orange juice or water

15 g/½ oz flaked almonds

2 small egg whites

100 g/3½ oz caster sugar

1 Preheat the oven to 200°C/ 400°F/ Gas Mark 6. Place each slice of ginger cake on an ovenproof plate and sprinkle with the ginger wine.

2 Quarter, core and slice the apple into a small saucepan. Add the chopped apricots and orange juice, and simmer the mixture over a low heat for 5 minutes, or until tender.

3 Stir the flaked almonds into the cooked fruit and spoon the mixture equally over the slices of soaked cake, piling it up in the centre.

4 Whisk the egg whites until very stiff and dry, then whisk in the sugar, a little at a time, making sure the meringue has become stiff again before adding the next quantity of sugar.

5 Either pipe or spread the meringue over the fruit and cake, making sure that both are completely covered.

6 Place in the preheated oven for 4–5 minutes, until golden. Serve hot.

Index